THE
PERFECT
LEADERSHIP
TRIAD

HOW TOP EXECUTIVES MAXIMIZE PRODUCTIVITY THROUGH PEOPLE, COACHING, AND PERFORMANCE

ERIC TURBIVILLE

TG Publishing

Published by TG Publishing
TG Publishing (USA) LLC, 5000 Eldorado Parkway, Frisco, Texas 75033, U.S.A.

First published in the United States of America by TG Publishing, LLC, 2020

THE LIBRARY OF CONGRESS HAS CATALOGED THE PAPERBACK EDITION AS FOLLOWS:
Turbiville, Eric.
The Perfect Leadership Triad: How top executives maximize productivity through people, coaching, and performance / by Eric Turbiville
p. cm.
Includes index
ISBN: 978-1-7346571-0-4
Leadership

Printed in the United State of America

Good leaders know what to do.

Great leaders know how to do things in a way that inspires people.

The greatest leaders are people-focused, coaching-centered, and performance-driven. These are the leaders who consistently shine above other leaders. They put people first and coach them so their people can grow, develop, and perform. These leaders are more than inspirational; they care about and respect their people.

I wrote this book for those who want to become the greatest leaders so they can transform how leaders impact employees and organizations. These are the leaders who leave an inspiring legacy.

For my mom, Barbara, who taught me to be a kind person and an avid learner; my inspiring wife, Randa; and my awesome children and energetic grandchildren. You inspire me and make me want to be better!

Contents

Introduction

Why People, Coaching, and Performance Matter

"Satisfied employees mean satisfied customers, which leads to profitability."

–Anne M. Mulcahy, *CEO of Xerox*

Based on my experience as a Fortune 500 executive and an executive coach, I believe that leaders must be people-focused, coaching-centered, and performance-driven. At the heart of leadership is caring about and respecting your employees. When leaders care about and respect their people, the employees will buy into the leader's vision, be more engaged, and work harder for them.

Leaders who truly put people first will find that business success will follow. Richard Branson, founder of the Virgin Group, said, "Clients do not come first. Employees come first. If you take care of your employees, they will take care of the clients." Your employees come before the business. They *are* your business. Without them you cannot create a great customer experience.

Great leaders are great coaches. They invest the time in coaching their people in order to inspire and mobilize them to achieve goals. The act of coaching people demonstrates the leader's commitment to help people grow and develop.

11

Coaching engenders trust and confidence between the leader and the employee she is coaching.

If leaders truly care about their people, they will hold them accountable. Leaders are responsible for the performance of their team. When leaders define and focus on the process of being successful, they will meet or exceed their goals. Great leaders set clear expectations and coach for performance. Leadership entails holding people accountable to meet expectations. At the core of performance-driven leadership is a company-wide culture of coaching and performance.

All organizations have a culture, whether positive or negative, and it is senior leadership's responsibility to be purposeful about creating and living it. Leaders shape the culture and the culture shapes the employees. When senior leaders purposefully create, develop, and nourish a positive culture, employees at all levels of the organization are affected. When leaders are not purposeful, a culture by default will be created. And this default culture may not be what you want it to be!

How would your people describe your culture? Do they even know you *have* a culture? As a leader, can you articulate that culture? Do you share this information with potential and current employees?

The first step in defining your culture is to go to the people who live it every day. Encourage your employees to tell you about the culture. If your employees cannot clearly articulate your culture, you have a problem.

People want to work for companies that have engaging leaders and cultures. They want to fit into the organization and wish to feel recognized and fulfilled when they work. At the end of the day, employees want to feel good about the work they do.

When I begin coaching an executive, the first thing I want to know is how she would describe the organization's culture. This gives me insight into the challenges I will face as a coach. The organizational culture, and the alignment of the executive's values with the organization's values, impacts how successful the executive and I will be in the coaching engagement.

We have all heard about great corporate cultures that have had a significant impact on employees, customers, and the business. We think about Disney, Starbucks, Southwest Airlines, and the Virgin Group. These companies have consistently created cultures that attract top talent because people love to work there.

At the center of these companies is a focus on the employees and consequently on the customers. The companies have created a customer experience that makes the employees feel great about their work. They feel great because they are treated respectfully and their employers care about them.

Now, more about becoming a people-focused, coaching-centered, and performance-driven leader....

1

The Perfect Leadership Triad

What are the biggest challenges that executives face in today's evolving business environment? According to a recent survey of CEOs, the failure to attract and retain top talent is the number one issue facing organizations.

So, how can leaders and organizations address this challenge? They can attract, engage, and retain key talent and then can maximize performance by establishing a people-focused culture that leverages high-impact coaching. They can establish a culture that hires and promotes leaders who value employees, coach their people to perform at high levels, and establish clear, high expectations of their teams.

At the heart of great leadership lies a people-focused, coaching-centered, and performance-driven approach. When leaders follow these three principles, they will develop a high-performing organization with a clear competitive advantage.

Three Questions Leaders Ask

A leader asks herself three vital questions:

1. Which comes first—my business, our customers, or my employees?

2. What is the most productive thing I can do to retain key employees and keep them engaged and motivated?

3. How can I maximize performance, profits, and productivity, all the while ensuring long-term success in a rapidly changing, dynamic marketplace?

You will find the answers to these important questions in the pages of this book.

My Leadership Journey

I spent 25 years as a leader and executive in the healthcare industry. I started leading teams in my twenties at a large, global healthcare conglomerate. I was a young leader with responsibilities over employees much older and more experienced than I. I learned early in my career that I did not have all the answers. I needed to listen to people who were much smarter and more knowledgeable than I.

I now realize that the most important lesson that I learned was that employees come before the business and shareholders. My approach was not always popular with my managers. I was accused of being soft and caring too much about my people, even though my teams were always top performers.

I had one manager tell me that I would never make it to the executive level because I "cared too much" about my people! Unfortunately, this is a typical response from business-focused leaders.

I want to be crystal clear about what I mean about "putting people first." Being a people-focused leader does not mean that you are best friends with your employees or that you do not hold them accountable for performance. In fact, if you *do* put your people first, you expect them to exceed expectations, and accordingly you help them along the path to success.

As a certified and credentialed executive coach and former executive, I have learned the importance of developing employees through coaching. Without effective coaching, employees will flounder and will not grow and progress. Both people development and performance coaching are critical to a leader's success. You cannot have long-term success without learning to be an effective coach.

Why I Decided to Be a Formal Leader

Have you ever worked for a manager who was so bad that you wanted to go into management yourself, as a way to block people like him from being promoted into management? Well, I have! Now, don't get me wrong. I have had a lot of great leaders in my career, but one particularly poor leader really stands out and affected my career path.

My initial motivation to become a formal leader and manager came from one of my first managers, who unfortunately stood out as a horrible example of someone trying to provide people-focused leadership. While I recognized some good leadership qualities in him, I learned more from the things I felt he did wrong.

His first mistake was focusing only on the business. This was obvious, because he never talked about anything *but* the business. He showed no interest in his subordinates, either personally or professionally. This caused the team to distrust him, because we felt that he didn't care about us.

The irony is that, while all he did was focus on the business, he was in fact not performance driven. He rarely spoke about our individual performance, and he never recognized or rewarded us for exceeding expectations. He had zero process to achieve the lofty goals that he set for our team. He just told us vague things like "go out there and get it done!"

He offered no coaching to help us improve. A day in the field or office with him was dreadful. When we were with customers, he simply watched. He never contributed anything to the conversation. After the customer meeting, he only focused on the negative things that happened. He offered no help to coach and develop us so that we could become more competent. As a result, over time we felt trapped and did not believe that we could grow and develop, primarily because we lacked his support.

We had to be careful, because if we shared ideas or thoughts with him, he took credit for them with his boss. This created an environment of distrust. There was no candor or sharing of ideas. He never acknowledged our contributions to the company or team. He was self-serving. He clearly loved himself, but we didn't feel the same way about him.

If you were one of his favorites, you were golden. If you were not—and I for one was not—you could count on even less support and help from him. Of course, those of us who were not his favorites could never trust him. Working under him was like having a bad experience with Santa Claus, where you wonder if he thinks you have been naughty or nice. I often pondered how I could get on my boss's nice list.

His one good quality was that he was a great motivator. In fact, he motivated me to get into management, principally because of all the management qualities that he lacked. I figured that if I myself became a leader, there would be one less leader who didn't care about or appreciate people. As I look back on that difficult year under his management, I am grateful for the lessons that I learned. I absorbed more from him about leadership do's and don'ts than from any other manager in my entire career. I learned that adverse experiences are *growing* experiences! And I learned that you must experience the bad to appreciate the good. Most importantly, I decided to become a people-focused leader.

Why Did *You* Become a Leader?

As I have spoken to leaders across many industries, I commonly hear that they typically get into management because they enjoy seeing people grow and develop. They love to help people reach their career and personal goals.

If this is the case, why are there so many leaders who fail to focus on this? Why do many of them care more about the business than their people? After all, it is not the business that grows the people; it is the people who grow the business.

One of the paradoxes of leadership is that the more you give to your people, the more you gain in return. When a leader develops talent, she gets increased employee productivity, builds trust, and creates a loyal employee.

So, why did *you* become a leader? This is an important question that you need to answer. The answer dictates your priorities and determines how you go about leading people. If you became a leader to develop and grow people, then do the things I will talk about in this book!

What Kind of Leader Are You?

For many years, those of us in the business world have heard about the importance of focusing on our employees' strengths. Hundreds of books have been published on focusing on employees, coaching them to success, and driving their performance. To my knowledge, no single leadership book has brought these principles together in one source. I will attempt to do so in these pages.

Many of the principles in this book will appear to be common sense. Unfortunately, as Voltaire said, "Common sense is not so common." Most leaders know "what to do." Great leaders know how to do it effectively and in ways that motivate people.

How you do things with your own people will determine your success as a leader.

If you know what you need to do as a leader, you are already 10 percent there! When you learn how to do it effectively, you begin the leadership journey. Leadership is an iterative process. No one has perfected this process. The best you can do as a leader is to improve every single day. As a former Fortune 500 executive, I am here to help you on this journey.

The first question you should ask yourself is: "What am I doing to build and maintain a high-performing team?" It is not enough to set aspirational goals and expectations to win. Leaders find, hire, coach, inspire, and reward the right people. They set clear and high expectations. Leaders ask great questions that will help them to develop the competencies and skills of each and every employee.

The second question you should ask yourself is: "How can I get to the next level and perform better and more effectively than I am doing now?" Leadership is all about people, coaching, and performance. If you take care of these three things, you will maximize performance and increase profits.

The third question you should ask yourself is: "Do I believe the business comes before the employee?" I have watched leaders and organizations struggle with this quandary throughout my entire career. Even companies that say they believe employees come first tend to fail to live by this principle. Wall Street and investors typically drive a short-term leadership mentality that demands that the business come before the employees.

This breeds organizational cultures where leaders are not trusted, employee engagement and retention are low, and performance is not sustained.

The final question leaders ask is: "What is the single most effective activity that I can do to build trust and develop a high-performing team?" Certainly, building trust by being a transparent and candid leader will help you along the path. The hard reality is that coaching and developing your people is the single most effective activity to drive performance. As you give back to each of your employees by coaching him, he will respond by trusting you, and will soon follow you and eventually perform at a higher level because he knows you care about him.

Are You a Dog-Kicking Boss?

I remember the first few months of my initial leadership position. After I got my feet wet by meeting my team, starting to know them individually, and beginning the process of developing mutual trust, my company sent me to an American Management Association first-line management course.

We did the usual activities, as we received all the pearls of wisdom that our instructor had learned in his career. I still recall the question that he asked all the new managers in the room: "What has been your greatest learning so far as a leader?"

As I pondered that question, I had an epiphany! It was a simple lesson. I had learned that as a leader I needed to recognize the power I had over my employees' lives. I do not mean this in an egotistical way, but rather as a practical principle. When I spent time with my people, how did they feel at the end of the day? Did I build trust with them? Did they feel inspired? Did I coach them? Did I clarify expectations so they could focus on the right things? Did I mobilize them to accomplish their goals? Or did they go home and just want to "kick the dog"?

As a leader, you must recognize the power you have over your employees' personal and professional lives. I am not talking about authority or position. Nor am I talking about ego. I am referring to the impact, either positive or negative, that a leader can have on her people.

I often ask other leaders if they think they are a "dog-kicking boss." Their answer to that question creates a greater understanding of their impact as a leader. Remember that every interaction you have with your people is an opportunity for you to build trust (by being people-focused), to coach and inspire them to become better (by acting as if they were coaching-centered), and to help them perform their job more effectively (by being performance-driven).

Three Elements of The Perfect Leadership Triad

"Triad" is defined as "a group or set of three connected things."

Leadership, you'll recall, is all about people, coaching, and performance. Establishing and living a people-focused, coaching-centered, and performance-driven leadership approach comprises what I call the Perfect Leadership Triad. All three elements are required if you wish to create a strong leadership culture. The culture is far less effective if you leave out even one of these elements.

I have had the opportunity to lead teams, some small and others large, for over 25 years. I have learned that the highest-performing leaders combine three elements of leadership that drives the business: they put employees before their customers and shareholders, they focus their efforts on coaching employees, and they consistently drive performance.

When your employees know that you care about and respect them, they will buy in to your vision, become more engaged, and work harder for you. Happy employees mean happy customers. Leaders *must* be people-focused if they want to experience long-term success.

Great leaders are coaching-centered. They recognize that coaching is the best way to gain trust and demonstrate their commitment to employees. It is also the most effective way to grow and develop their people. When leaders coach employees, they receive more in return than the employees do. The result is a more competent, more engaged, and happier employee— *and* a successful leader.

High-performing leaders care enough about their employees to hold them accountable. Performance-driven leadership stands at the heart of all high-performing organizations. Organizations that actively maintain coaching cultures are twice as likely to be high-performing.

Senior leaders like you determine whether a company is good or great. One of their principal responsibilities is to create a leadership culture that believes in, trusts, coaches, and also sets high, clear expectations of every employee. There is no substitute for a people-focused, coaching-centered, and performance-driven leader!

People-Focused Leadership

"Your employees come first. And if you treat your employees right, guess what? Your customers come back, and that makes your shareholders happy. Start with employees and the rest follows from that."

–**Herb Kelleher,** *former CEO and Cofounder of Southwest Airlines*

"If we win the hearts and minds of employees, we're going to have better business success."

–**Mary Barra**, *CEO of General Motors*

The Perfect Leadership Triad starts with recognizing that your business is created by and maximized by your people. Without them, you are only an empty shell of a company.

When I speak of your need to be people-focused, I am not necessarily referring to being close to your employees. I am referring to genuinely caring about them enough to be candid with them in your management, to coach them regularly, and always to hold them accountable.

Leaders should never be people-focused at the expense of customers and the company. Rather, leaders become customer-centric by being people-focused, so that the company reaps financial rewards.

Most companies and leaders do not put their people first. This may be because they do not actually believe in their people or have not trained and coached them to be effective. Maybe they believe that their product or service can sell itself on its own merits. Perhaps they think that as management they can get everything they need out of the people that they need to be successful. Maybe they imagine that they as leaders drive the business through their leadership, regardless of how they treat the employees. Or they believe that people will respond by simply being told what to do. Many leaders treat people like robots, expecting them to be programmed on how to execute their job responsibilities.

Many leaders and organizations do not even try to win the hearts and minds of their employees. People are not coached and developed, so eventually they will become disenchanted and leave. In fact, employees' loyalty to the company is not reciprocated by the company to the employee. This is one of the reasons that Gallup has found that about 70 percent of employees are disengaged at work; their hearts are simply not connected to their job. (Source: Jim Harter, "Employee Engagement on the Rise in the U.S.," gallup.com)

I will talk more about being a people-focused leader in chapter 2.

Coaching-Centered Leadership

Great leadership begins with effective coaching. Coaching is the single most impactful activity that a leader can do to improve performance and profits. It generates trust and learning between leaders and employees. Most leaders enjoy developing and growing employees. The best way to accomplish this is through effective, thoughtful coaching. Leaders perform best when they dedicate time to coaching their employees—and when they see the employees responding to that coaching.

Coaching is a two-way street between the leader and the employee. It takes both parties to ensure that coaching is effective. Both the leader and the employee *must* be coachable.

But why does coaching make such a positive difference? It happens because employees appreciate a leader's effort to help them. The goodwill creates a bond of trust between the leader and the employee. Employees reciprocate the efforts of the leader by working harder for her to ensure that she is successful.

Chapters 3, 4, and 5 are focused on coaching-centered leadership.

Performance-Driven Leadership

As a leader, I always cared enough about my employees to hold them accountable. I knew that my having high performance expectations of each employee would almost always lead to that higher performance.

As discussed in greater detail in the next chapter, all great leaders set high, clear expectations, including the expectation that each employee will meet performance goals. They also ensure that every employee understands his contribution to the team. Metrics are set and measured for every key performance indicator. Everyone in the organization is expected to achieve their personal goals.

It is critical to remember that performance is driven through coaching. Coaching results in higher performance, especially when it is based on people-development.

I will talk more about performance-driven leadership in chapter 6.

The Perfect Leadership Triad Culture

> *"Culture is not the most important thing in the world. It's the only thing. It is the thing that drives the business."*
>
> –**Jim Sinegal**, *founder and former CEO, Costco*

Leadership happens within an organization's culture. Leaders set the tone for the entire organization through their behaviors. Leaders determine the culture. Employees respond differently to each type of leadership approach. An organization's performance is usually directly correlated with leaders' behaviors.

When leaders combine all three elements of The Perfect Leadership Triad, they can create and build high-performing teams. The key to a great culture is making an ingrained commitment to the triad.

I will talk more about a company's culture in chapter 9.

Conclusion

As you will see in this book, the results of being people-focused, coaching-centered, and performance-driven are higher performance, increased employee engagement, and greater retention of key employees. Happy employees will help you develop and retain happy customers who are likely to use more of your products or services in the future.

New and experienced leaders are guided by these three elements of leadership if they are to sustain long-term success. At its base, leadership is about people, coaching, and performance.

Ask yourself these questions about your leadership values and style:

» Why did I become a leader?

» What motivates and inspires me as a leader?

» What kind of leader do I want to be?

» Do I believe that employees come before the customers?

» If so, how do I demonstrate this to my people?

» Am I a great coach?

» How am I currently coaching my people so they can be more productive and successful?

» If I am not an effective coach, what can I do to become one?

» What expectations do I have for my people?

» How clearly am I communicating these expectations?

» How am I holding my people accountable for their performance?

2

People-Focused Leadership

You want us to care about company growth?
How about you care about your people first!

Employees are the most important asset. *Wrong!* People are not assets. They are human beings. People are the core of your business!

Employees follow and trust leaders who genuinely care about them. In fact, I have learned that people will work harder for you, buy into your vision, and follow your leadership if they know you care about and respect them.

Many leaders believe that the business comes before its people. Wrong again! The people *are* the business! Richard Branson said, "Clients do not come first. Employees come first. If you take care of your employees, they will take care of the clients."

Another leader remarked, "If you exceed the expectations of your employees, they will consistently exceed the expectations of your customers."

31

I would add, "Treat your people better than your customers, and your customers will treat you better than your competitors."

So, What does this mean to you as a leader? You must recognize that people drive your business. So your focus is on leading and coaching your people. You develop a culture of trust, respect, candor, honesty, and transparency. At the center of most great companies is the recognition that employees are vital for their success. In fact, your people are a key source of sustainable competitive advantage.

Attributes of a People-Focused Leader

> *"Leadership is all about people. It is not about organizations. It is not about plans. It is not about strategies. It is all about people motivating people to get the job done. You have to be people-centered."*
>
> **–Colin Powell,** *former U.S. Secretary of State*

Because people are the most important part of an organization, people-focused leadership is required to ensure success. When an organization prioritizes the importance of employees, its productivity, retention, engagement, and revenue all invariably increase.

People-focused leaders put employees first. They recognize that people come before the business, their customers, and even Wall Street. This is counterintuitive for most leaders and organizations—especially for Wall Street!

Costco Wholesale, a global membership warehouse club, is a great example of a people-focused organization with high wages, good benefits, and many internal growth opportunities. Despite ongoing pressure from Wall Street and investors to reduce its wages and benefits, Costco adheres to the principles and values that have made it successful. In fact, Costco leaders believe that its high wages and benefits lead to greater retention (94 percent) and higher productivity. I will say more about Costco as an example of a people-focused organization later in this chapter.

People-focused leaders demonstrate their commitment to their employees by investing time and focus in coaching them. Coaching has many benefits, including building mutual trust. As leaders help to develop the competencies and skills of their employees, they model the importance of a coaching culture. A focus on coaching is highly correlated with business performance, employee engagement, and retention. (Josh Bersin, "High-Impact Talent Management: Trends, Best Practices and Industry Solutions," May 2007, joshbersin.com)

Leaders recognize that every touch point and coaching moment provides an opportunity to listen, teach, and inspire. In fact, each employee interaction, when combined with the behaviors of the leader, is a chance to increase mutual trust.

At Novo Nordisk, a global healthcare company headquartered in Denmark, Andy Ajello, its former senior vice president of Diabetes and Obesity Sales, set the bar high for leaders. His beliefs that leaders should "lead people first" and that the leaders should "know details about employees and their families" established a tone of people-focused leadership. He followed General Norman Schwarzkopf's philosophy that a leader's job is to take care of the troops.

Ajello added that his leadership team always conveyed to their employees the message that "we trust you!" Like most great leaders, he believes that "actions are more important than words." Each year he personally sends a handwritten note to the top 145 sales performers, thanking them for their contributions. He is always candid with the sales team, often keeping them updated on home office decisions. He believes that you demonstrate authenticity by the candid stories that you share. As a result of his vulnerable and transparent approach, he built trust with the sales force—and his leaders emulated his behavior.

Leaders are honest, candid, and even vulnerable. The benefits of this type of leadership include building trust and confidence among your people. Vulnerable leaders breed employee loyalty and inspire greater performance. Candid leaders earn the respect and admiration of employees. And people-focused leaders demonstrate through their behavior what employees desire—a leader who is "real."

People-focused leaders trust their employees, yet hold them accountable for performance. When employees commit to action, the leader always follows up with the question "How will I know it is *done*?" Leaders give employees the autonomy to do the job in the manner they choose, while expecting them to return and report with updates on the actions they committed to take.

Finally, people-focused leaders and organizations alike recognize that focusing on employees and developing a strong, people-based culture gives them a huge competitive advantage. The reasons are simple: happy, engaged employees lead to happy customers. And happy customers lead to increased revenue.

People-focused cultures are full of motivated employees who believe in and live the values of the company. Such employees are loyal and dedicated to the success of the organization. They hold themselves accountable for performance and thrive in an environment where leaders are candid, trustworthy, and, again, "real."

In my research, I have unfortunately found very few companies that are good at putting people first. Most companies are too shortsighted to act on the belief that their employees are critical for their success. When companies *do* focus on employees, then productivity, retention, and revenues increase.

People-Focused Leaders Create Stronger, More Cohesive Cultures

> *"Employees who believe that management is concerned about them as a whole person—not just an employee—are more productive, more satisfied, more fulfilled. Satisfied employees mean satisfied customers, which leads to profitability."*
>
> **–Anne Mulcahy**, *CEO of Xerox*

But why *is* a people-focused culture actually more productive? Leaders who respect and care about their people create and maintain a positive, trust-based culture where employees can thrive and develop.

A strong, people-focused culture requires that all the leaders within it actually live that culture. If a leader behaves in a way that is not congruent with the culture, she must be coached, counseled, and given feedback. If she does not correct her behaviors, she should be removed so that she does not cause further damage to the culture of the organization.

Southwest Airlines—A People-Focused Company

One fine example of an organization that is people-focused is Southwest Airlines. Cofounder Herb Kelleher set the tone that his employees are more important than the customers. He understood the concept that if you take care of your employees, they will take care of the customers.

The principal values of Southwest Airlines are to "Live and Work the Southwest Way." To do that, employees are expected to have a Servant's Heart, a Warrior Spirit, and a Fun-LUVing attitude (yes, corny, but effective).

Their purpose is to "Connect People to what's important in their lives through friendly, reliable, and low-cost air travel." When the company began in 1967, cofounder and presently the former CEO Herb Kelleher set out to create a low-cost airline that competed with commercial bus services.

Gregg Gregory shares a telling story about the culture at Southwest Airlines. He was on a flight about 15 years ago.

Herb Kelleher himself boarded the plane early in the process, walked to the very last row, and selected a middle seat. Those who know the boarding process on Southwest know that is a very unusual seat selection. Most people are looking for an aisle or window seat near the front of the plane. (Southwest saves money by not reserving specific seats in advance.)

During the flight, Kelleher was speaking with the flight attendants and began helping them serve drinks and peanuts. What a great example of a humble leader with a servant's heart! Despite his rank, seniority, and prime position in the company, he modeled what it means to serve the customer. It demonstrated his commitment to the people at Southwest Airlines; he was willing to do everything, however great or small, that he asked the employees to do. This is a company that still today truly lives a people-focused culture at all levels of the organization.

Herb Kelleher said this about the spirit at Southwest Airlines in an interview with *Investor Daily:* "the core of our success: That's the most difficult thing for a competitor to imitate. They can buy all the physical things. The things you can't buy are dedication, devotion, loyalty—the feeling you are participating in a crusade." (Excerpts from Ekatrina Walter, "In One Plane Ride, the Co-Founder of Southwest Airlines Teaches Us a Powerful Leadership Lesson," *Inc.,* July 10, 2017, https://www. inc.com/ekaterina-walter/a-simple-but-powerful-leadership-lesson-from-the-co-founder-of-southwest-airline.html

People-Focused Leaders Improve Performance, Engagement, and Retention

> *"The real competitive advantage in any business is one word only, which is 'people.'"*
>
> –**Kamil Toume**, *author*

Trust engenders higher performance. I will repeat this: *When people know you care about and respect them, they will work harder for you.* It seems like a simple principle. The converse is true, too. If people know you don't care about them, they not only will feel disrespected but they will do the bare minimum and be mediocre. They will spend their time complaining and looking for a new job instead of working. They will be disengaged. They will quit emotionally while nominally staying with your organization.

Clearly, exceptions to this can be found with consistent high performers, but the questions to ask are: "If the leader really *did* care about and respect them, would they put in extra effort?" "Could they perform at an even higher level?" The average B player on your team will become a C player under a leader who is not people-focused.

If you are *not* people-focused, do not plan on being successful in the long term. True, you may experience some wins and achievements, but you are missing an opportunity to excel at your highest performance as a leader. You are forgoing an opportunity to be consistently successful. If you want to drive better performance throughout your organization, think about how you might become more people-focused (and inspire your direct reports to become the same).

"Effective leaders create positive cultures. This makes it possible for ordinary employees to accomplish extraordinary goals. A worldwide study of the auto industry, for example, confirmed that those applying people-centered practices were twice as productive and had significantly higher levels of quality as those who favored more traditional mass production. A one degree standard deviation improvement in human resources practices produced $20,000-$40,000 increase in stock market value per employee. Brokerage firms that improved broker retention by 10%, increased broker value by 155%. Watson Wyatt, respected human resource consulting firm, concluded that 'companies that link employee development to business strategy have 40% higher total shareholder returns than companies that do not.'" (Jack Zenger, "By the Numbers: Superior Leadership Produces Higher Return than Superior Talent," *Forbes,* October 31, 2014)

In organizations and teams that are people-focused, engagement and retention are both considerably higher. Why does this happen? Leaders understand that how they treat people determines each employee's sense of belonging and motivation.

I have seen organizations that at one time had a strong sense of focusing on people but that lost it with a new leader. Although the new leader had a strong sense of why the company existed and how to execute the strategy, he did not focus on the employees, thereby decreasing their performance, engagement, and ultimately retention.

A people-focused approach provides a sustainable competitive advantage that is difficult to copy. It is embedded in the very purpose of the organization. It is established and reinforced by the most senior leader, whose example casts a wide leadership shadow over the company's other leaders.

How Do You Know if You Are People-Focused?

"Our philosophy is that happy and engaged employees produce happy customers, as employee engagement lies at the heart of good customer experience. If you want your customers to feel supported, valued, and heard, you must first ensure your front-line employees feel supported, valued, and heard."

–**Paul Segre**, *former CEO of Genesys*

So ask yourself: Do you genuinely care about the employees you lead? Do you want them to be successful? Are you willing to coach them and help them succeed? Are your behaviors and actions congruent with these beliefs? If so, you are probably a people-focused leader.

Consistency and congruency in your actions and attitudes are paramount to demonstrating your belief system to your own team. For example, in a crisis do your actions and behaviors change? When you are stressed or feeling pressure from your boss, especially about performance issues, do you take it out on your team? If the answer to either question is yes, you are not consistently being people-focused.

Listening is another indicator that you are people-focused. A great leader should listen more than he talks. It is important that, while you are listening, you not be crafting your next comment or suggestion. You must be laser-focused on what is being said and on showing genuine concern about it and interest in it. When leaders do not listen, employees disengage and eventually lose trust in and respect for the leader.

Does your team trust you? If they do, you are doing something right. Do you know why they trust you? You can be sure that it is your beliefs, behaviors, candor, and actions that have led to the development of this trust. You have proven to your team that you are trustworthy. Be careful with trust, though; while it takes a lot of time to build trust, one incongruent action on your part can destroy it.

Do you treat all people respectfully, or just those above you with more impressive titles? Again citing Herb Kelleher, Southwest Airlines' cofounder, who said: "One piece of advice that always stuck in my mind is that people should be respected and trusted as people, not because of their position or title."

If you hold your people accountable, you are being people-focused. It shows that you care about them, because you want them to be successful. It also shows that you have made a commitment to the organization *and* the team to accomplish what you have been asked to do as a leader.

Conducting "Stay Interviews"

Do you know why employees remain with your company? Have you ever asked your employees why they stay with you? You might be surprised at the answers! I have found that a Stay Interview offers a gateway into the minds of your employees that will shed light on what you are doing right...and what you can improve.

When I conduct a Stay Interview, I start with the highest performers. These are the people who will help you understand why they want to continue to be associated with you and your company.

For the interview, it is critical that you get them out of the typical work environment. Take them to lunch or for coffee. They will feel more comfortable and will be more likely to be honest with you. Make sure you establish an environment of trust for the conversation. Be vulnerable and honest about what you are trying to achieve with it.

Ask them, "What do you like *most* about working here?" Listen. Then listen harder. The answer to this question will help you understand what you are doing right both as a leader and as an organization. It will shed light about your culture and how it is influencing your employees. You will clearly see from the answer if the employee really understands the purpose of your organization.

Then ask "What keeps you working here?" This question reveals more about what the employee likes about her job, but, more importantly, what you are doing that engages her. Do you perhaps inspire her as a leader? Does she enjoy working with her teammates? Maybe the culture and vision of the company are among the things that motivate her to stay. But be careful if an employee says she stays "because of the money" or because she has a family to support. You must dig deeper to see what her internal motivators are so that you can understand her other motivators.

Follow up this question with another one: "What do you like *least* about working here?" You will quickly find out what you need to improve. It will reveal where the weaknesses and potential blind spots are in your leadership or in the larger organization.

Ask, "If you could change something about your job, what would that be?" This transfers the power to the employee to correct any problems. As a leader, with that question you are both empowering and encouraging the employee to help you solve the problem—*and* you are creating trust with the employee.

"What talents are not being used in your current role?" This question helps reveal the skills and abilities of the employee that she does not feel you are recognizing or leveraging. It may reveal that she would be a better fit in another role or perhaps that she has the ability to take on more responsibility.

"What would you like to learn here?" The second leading cause of employees' leaving a job is the lack of growth and development they see in their position. The best way to grow and develop is through experiential learning. Maybe the employee wants to grow in order to be promoted and take on more responsibilities. Many employees are not looking for upward mobility but rather for in-band promotions. There are also instances when the employee is looking to further their formal education through university or other types of classes.

Once you recognize their learning opportunities and hear about their career ambitions, you can ask, "What can I do to best support you?" This question can also be used to uncover other opportunities for you to support the employee. For instance, if the employee is up for an in-band or upward promotion, she may ask for your endorsement of her candidacy.

"What can I do more of, or less of, as your manager?" This is a vital question for any leader. It is the equivalent of a "start, stop, and continue" exercise. If you have listened carefully throughout the Stay Interview and verbally acknowledged the feedback the employee has given you, she will be honest with you. What you hear may not be what you want to hear! Be prepared for the employee to reveal things that you were not expecting.

A final question empowers the employee to think like a CEO or owner: "If you owned or led this company, what would you change?" Ask the question and then listen. You may hear ideas that you instinctively know would not work or just may not make sense to you. By contrast, the employee may provide insights and thoughts that will help you as a leader or help the company. Never underestimate the thinking and ideas generated by the employee!

It is critical that you reflect on and then act on the feedback received in the Stay Interview. By doing so, not only will you build trust with your employees, you will also show that you are truly listening and taking action.

For more information on the Stay Interview or to get a copy of the questions, please go to **turbivillegroup.com.**

Costco Case Study

Since opening in 1983 in Seattle, Washington, Costco set out with a value system that consisted of being employee-focused, being committed to quality, and encouraging its employees to show an entrepreneurial spirit.

Costco now has over 90 million members and over 231,000 employees, with 135,000 of them working for branches in the United States. The net sales of the company have grown from $87 billion in 2011 to $138 billion in 2018.

Costco has been able to sustain these values throughout the years, even with a change in leadership in 2012 from the cofounder and former CEO, Jim Sinegal, to the current CEO, Walter Craig Jelinek.

Costco Values

1. Take care of employees, customers, and suppliers first.

2. Do the right thing.

3. Provide opportunities for employee growth, development, and promotion.

4. Enforce gender equality.

Costco's people-focused leadership approach—a differentiator when compared to that of most other Fortune 500 companies—is demonstrated by its relatively high wages, as compared to those offered by competitors, as well as its excellent benefits, extensive developmental opportunities, and a culture that attracts and retains talented employees. Even when Wall Street opposed Costco's "high wages," the CEO held his ground. He said these high wages and opportunities given to employees to develop and grow were among the reasons Costco does so well. As previously stated, its mantra is "people before business."

One way the company demonstrates a people-focused leadership approach is its focus on an entrepreneurial drive for excellence. Having the autonomy to try new things gives the management team—and even the warehouse employees—room to find ways to exceed customer expectations.

A 2005 *New York Times* article stated:

"Combining high quality with stunningly low prices, [Costco products] appeal to upscale customers—and epitomize why some retail analysts say Mr. Sinegal just might be America's shrewdest merchant since Sam Walton.

"But not everyone is happy with Costco's business strategy. Some Wall Street analysts assert that Mr. Sinegal is overly generous not only to Costco's customers but to its workers as well.

"Costco's average pay, for example, is $17 an hour, 42 percent higher than its fiercest rival, Sam's Club. And Costco's health plan makes those at many other retailers look Scroogish. One analyst, Bill Dreher of Deutsche Bank, complained last year that at Costco 'it's better to be an employee or a customer than a shareholder.'

"Mr. Sinegal begs to differ. He rejects Wall Street's assumption that to succeed in discount retailing, companies must pay poorly and skimp on benefits, or must ratchet up prices to meet Wall Street's profit demands.

"Good wages and benefits are why Costco has extremely low rates of turnover and theft by employees, he said. And Costco's customers, who are more affluent than other warehouse store shoppers, stay loyal because they like that low prices do not come at the workers' expense. 'This is not altruistic,' he said. 'This is good business.'" (Steven Greenhouse, "How Costco Became the Anti-Wal-Mart," *New York Times,* July 17, 2005)

While Costco's people-focused approach resonates with its customers and employees alike, Wall Street fails to understand the connection between people and business. Costco has figured out that when employees are happy, feel challenged, and have autonomy in their job, they will exceed the customers' expectations. When customers are happy, revenue will increase. Happy employees lead to higher engagement and productivity.

Additionally, employee retention is improved, as evidenced by Costco's low turnover rate.

Anyone who predicted a change in the culture as a result of Wall Street's comments was flat wrong. Craig Jelinek, Costco's president and chief executive officer since 2012, has continued the values of the founders. As of 2020, Costco continues to pay great wages, supplies medical coverage for its employees at reasonable rates, and provides them with developmental and promotional opportunities.

Lessons Learned from Costco

In a people-focused culture, employees buy into the vision and then live the values of the culture because they feel energized by them.

People-focused companies give employees the autonomy to make decisions and be the doers of the "What." They allow employees to decide how to execute.

While people-focused companies recognize that each employee owns his own development, they provide opportunities for employees to grow and develop. For Costco, this means that *only* internal employees are promoted to leadership positions.

Great companies spend a lot of time ensuring that employees have opportunities to develop on the job. They create opportunities for them to take on additional responsibilities, be trained, be coached, and have new experiences. These opportunities and experiences are not just for high-potential employees; they are for each and every employee.

Finally, employees need to be heard and appreciated to feel connected to the company. Even if they do not have a vote in management actions, they appreciate their voices' being heard. Costco is one example of a company that listens to and often acts on the ideas of its employees.

Costco Results

The results for Costco are clear: Its employee retention rate is a whopping 94 percent, which leads to higher productivity and performance. This is far above the retention rate for competitors such as Walmart, Sam's Club, and Target.

Every Costco employee generates three times the revenue of a similar Walmart or Target employee, according to Investopedia. And Costco stock has grown at an average rate of 15 to 16 percent per year, over the last three decades. (Arturo Garcia, Born2Invest, March 11, 2018)

Conclusion

Being people-focused takes time and effort. It requires taking a disciplined and deliberate approach with employees.

When leaders and organizations are people-focused, they gain a sustainable competitive advantage. They set a tone that breeds trust and loyalty. Their candor is appreciated and reciprocated by employees. And they are respected by their employees.

People-focused leaders spend time learning how to be better coaches so they can help their employees achieve their goals. Coaching-centered leadership is the focus of the next chapter.

Ask yourself these questions about being a people-focused leader:

» What are my core values?

» How do I use every touch point and coaching moment as an opportunity to listen to, teach, and then inspire my people?

» What am I doing to be candid and vulnerable with my people, so that I can establish both trust and rapport with them?

» What am I doing to balance a people-focused approach with driving their best performance?

» How can my people-focused leadership approach create a competitive advantage for me as a leader?

» Why do employees stay with my company—and with me as a leader?

» How well do I listen to my employees?

» Which growth and developmental opportunities do I provide for my employees?

3

Coaching-Centered Leadership

"I absolutely believe that people, unless coached, never reach their maximum capabilities."

–Bob Nardelli, *former CEO of Home Depot*

Coaching is like leadership; it is both an iterative process and a journey. Coaching affects one employee at a time, so it takes time, patience, and a desire to be coached for the employee to develop and improve. Coaching requires two things: a leader who knows how to effectively coach and an employee who is coachable.

Two types of coaching can be employed. What we often think of is performance coaching, which is tactical and results-based. The other type of coaching is partnership coaching, which is more strategic and focuses on personal development. Both are required to successfully coach an employee.

Employees own their development. This means they are responsible for taking full advantage of opportunities to develop and grow. Leaders, by contrast, are accountable for their team's development. Ultimately, the success or failure of an employee falls on the shoulders of the leader. Therefore, it makes sense that that leader should be motivated to coach and develop the employees.

Employees will remember that a company controls their job, but the employees control their own career. Employees should learn, develop, and grow their skills and relationships, because they take these with them if they choose to leave an organization. With this in mind, leaders cannot be concerned if an employee chooses to leave. What they should care about is whether they coached and developed the employee to ensure that she is not leaving because of a lack of opportunity to develop and grow her career.

If an employee chooses to leave, the leader should take the mirror test. He asks himself the question, "Did I do everything I could to coach, teach, and develop this employee?" It is imperative that the leader is brutally honest with himself. If he failed, he does an immediate course-correction and seeks help from his boss to improve his coaching skills.

Coaching Is Highly Correlated with Performance

According to the international consulting services firm Deloitte, "The second management practice that drives engagement is coaching. A coaching culture is the practice that's most highly correlated with business performance, employee engagement, and overall retention. When new managers are promoted to supervisory positions, they often think their job is to direct or evaluate people. While directed management is important, it plays a smaller role than one might think. It is the coaching and development role of management that is the most valuable."

But one might ask "What makes a great coach? As Marcus Buckingham describes the role, great coaches understand people's strengths, move them into positions and rearrange work to leverage these strengths, and coach them to build on these strengths. Nothing makes a person feel better about work than being able to be highly successful." (Josh Bersin, "Becoming Irresistible: A New Model for Employee Engagement," *Deloitte Review* issue 16, January 27, 2015, https://www2.deloitte.com/insights/us/en/deloitte-review/issue-16/employee-engagement-strategies.html)

Providing Feedback Is Different from Coaching

Leaders are willing to provide both positive, affirming feedback and negative, constructive feedback. There is a time and place for coaching and a time and place for feedback. Great leaders know when to use each one.

Leaders can sometimes be puzzled about the differences between feedback and coaching. Here are a few:

Coaching is based on inquiry and questioning, while feedback is about telling an employee what they are doing right or wrong. A great coach asks catalytic questions that help an employee think and solve problems more effectively. A great leader provides feedback to employees, so they know what is going well and what is not going well.

Coaching focuses on helping employees reach their potential through growth opportunities and learning to ask the right questions. Feedback focuses more on telling the employee what and how to do things. This is especially true with new or inexperienced leaders.

Coaching is future-oriented and prepares an employee to think differently so she acts and behaves differently. It is about growth and development. Feedback is focused on the past or current behavior. Feedback helps an employee understand what she did right or wrong. It is corrective.

Coaching is about helping employees grow and develop. It focuses on developmental needs. Feedback focuses on corrective actions that must be taken to avoid failure. It focuses more on the negative than the positive. It is about making adjustments and doing course corrections, not making wholesale change.

Finally, *coaching is all about performance.* It is about seeing the possibility of success. Feedback focuses on the expected behaviors of the employee. Feedback is action-oriented, based on the expectations of the organization and leader.

The reality I faced when I implemented a coaching culture in one organization was that very few of its leaders were coaching. Instead, they were providing feedback and just telling employees what to do. They were neither giving their direct reports autonomy nor helping them think about their work performance more effectively. As a result, they were simply *not* coaching.

It took a significant amount of time and education for me to move these leaders toward coaching. After I established the expectation that leaders would coach, and then taught them how to do so effectively, I was gratified to see most of them adopting the new approach. Two early adopters, leaders who believed in and were passionate about coaching, even emerged to help encourage the team to coach more effectively. The result: the formation of a true coaching culture.

So, how do you balance feedback and coaching? Let me give you an example.

I had a first-line leader who was struggling to interpret marketing direction and communicate it to his team. The direction he was providing was not guiding his team to execute the strategy and increase revenues. His team was floundering.

The second-line leader recognized what was happening and provided feedback to this leader. Both the leaders knew things were not going well. Based on the feedback, the leader recognized that he did not clearly understand the marketing strategy, and as a result he was communicating ineffectively to his team. The second-line leader clarified the marketing strategy and then coached this leader on how to communicate it to his team and execute it.

Based on the feedback from his supervisor, the first-line leader recognized what he was doing wrong and clearly communicated the marketing strategy to his team. Additionally, the second-line leader effectively coached this leader so he could identify future needs and learn to think more effectively. The first-line leader developed from this experience and went on to be successful and even to become a second-line leader.

Situational Coaching

Every situation is different for a coach. In some cases, the employee is experienced in the subject and has a good idea what needs to be done. At the other extreme is a new or inexperienced employee who needs considerably more help and coaching.

In the first case, the leader can coach the employee without much need to instruct, teach, and tell. For example, an employee who has been working in a department for a few years and is given a new project that she is familiar with will not need a leader to direct and tell her everything she needs to do. Instead, the leader can ask questions that will help the employee find better solutions and successfully complete the project.

In the latter case, the leader will need to do a combination of coaching, telling, and providing feedback to help the employee be successful. If the employee genuinely does not understand how or what to do, it is critical that the leader intervenes to provide direction. Once the direction is followed, the leader needs to follow up with feedback on how the employee performed. In this case, feedback is especially important because the leader is helping the employee understand and learn how to be more effective and to grow her competencies.

The leader will coach the employee along the way to help her think more effectively so that she will learn from the experience. In this case, coaching is more rudimentary and basic, yet still a critical component of the employee's learning and development process. If a leader wants to build up an employee so she will not be dependent on the leader, effective coaching is the most important element of that process. It is what creates an independent and empowered employee.

I once had an employee who was fairly new to filling a second-line leadership position. While he was competent in his previous position, he struggled when leading leaders. He did not know what to do. What made the situation worse was that his previous leader had conditioned him to be overly reliant by telling the employee every little thing to do. The leader missed the critical element of providing feedback and then coaching the employee in ways that could help him to grow and become independent of the leader.

What I discovered was the need to balance telling this second-line leader how to perform the actions that he clearly did not know how to do, by offering good feedback and ample coaching. In this case, I let him experience some minor failures with his people and the directions he was giving them.

For example, at one point he changed his departmental strategy twice in a one-month period. This confused both his leaders and their direct reports. This caused their performance to drop off for a short time.

When he explained his new strategy to me, I provided feedback on how confusing this approach likely was to his team members. He responded positively to the feedback and made a few necessary course corrections.

A critical part of the feedback I provided to him was that he was missing an important element of leading: listening to his employees and then leveraging their knowledge, experience, and wisdom. He followed up with his leaders and explained his thinking to them. He also asked them to provide feedback on the strategy that they thought the department should follow.

With his leaders' feedback and ideas in place, I coached him so he himself could implement their thoughts and create a more effective departmental strategy. During the coaching process, he leaned on me to tell him the "correct" answer for the strategy. Since I knew that there is no perfect strategy for any department, I did not tell him what to do, as this would only cause dependence on me. What I did do was share my thoughts on the strategy and suggest effective ways of executing it.

With all this information, feedback, instruction, and coaching, he created a strong strategy and executed it. This case reinforced my conviction that leaders balance telling employees what and how to do things, instead providing feedback and coaching for their development and performance.

Peer Coaching

One of the most underutilized resources in companies is the practice of peer coaching. Learning from each of your colleagues' challenges and opportunities is a great way to learn to coach and even to *be* coached.

Peer coaching can be done formally or informally. My experience is that a formal peer coaching approach is more effective. As an executive, in one case I paired up my direct reports for a three-month period. Every three months I would rotate partners. The expectation was that they would spend at least one hour with each other every month.

I assured the leaders that they could choose the topic on which they wanted coaching from their peer, based on their current challenges or opportunities. This approach created far more trust and confidence in each other, brought our team together emotionally, provided the leaders with another leader's perspective, and in the end proved to be a real-life example of fine coaching, while also reinforcing the importance of coaching and helping our team be more effective at their jobs. I find peer coaching to be a valuable process that helps leaders grow, learn, and develop.

Autonomy: Let Your People Be the Doers of the What

"Don't tell people how to do things; tell them what to do and let them surprise you with their results."
–General George S. Patton Jr.

Leaders sometimes make the mistake of believing that everything must be done *their way*. To encourage real autonomy, leaders need to release that belief and let employees figure out how to do things after the Why and the What are communicated to them.

The more you trust your people to make good decisions, the more empowered they will feel to do the job. Your people will become more likely to step up and try new things. Employees who trust leaders are more likely to exceed expectations. And leaders who empower employees and hold them accountable will most likely exceed expectations.

When I took over the team that I previously discussed was struggling with coaching employees, I could have stamped my iron fist on the table and told them to start coaching and to stop disempowering employees by telling them everything to do.

Instead, I created a plan to help them become better coaches. The first thing I did was to demonstrate that I was trustworthy and that I had their best interests in mind. I truly wanted them to be successful. So I gave them autonomy to run their departments and teams. This developed a mutual trust between us.

I shared with them why the organization was doing what we were doing and what needed to be accomplished to be successful both as an organization and as a team. I let them decide how to do things. I gave them real autonomy.

I set clear, high expectations of the leaders and also their teams. I made it clear that everyone was expected to meet or exceed organizational goals. I showed them that I cared enough about them to expect high performance.

I then helped them to understand the impact of coaching employees and to appreciate how that coaching could assist in the development of their employees and the ultimate success of the organization.

As I will discuss in the next section, I allowed them to fail, and I supported and coached them when they did have setbacks.

The result of this approach was that the leaders felt empowered and recognized that they were developing into stronger leaders. The team went on to be not only successful, but also influential leaders within the organization.

Autonomy: Let Your People Fail

Coaching-centered leaders give people autonomy. They let them try new approaches and take on new challenges. A culture of "fail-fast, fail-forward" enables team members to struggle, grow, and develop.

I have had several direct reports in my career move in a direction that I knew would result in failure. I asked a lot of questions of them, to try to understand their thinking, and ultimately I let them make the decision. When they realized the decision was not effective, that created a coaching moment for the employee.

Steve Jobs, a founder of Apple, was well known for creating a culture in which failure was celebrated. It is difficult to be innovative without "failing your way forward" to achieve it.

One author reported, "Success does not breed success. It breeds failure. It is failure that breeds success." (D. G. Kolb, *Journal of Management Inquiry* 12 (2003): 180–83)

With that in mind, leaders should approach failures as a learning experience. Failures provide a great opportunity to coach and to help team members learn and grow. We are the sum total of our responses to all the challenges and opportunities we encounter in life. This includes failures. The more varied the experiences we have, the broader our perspective becomes.

I once had an employee who was convinced that his strategy to target the right market segment for a product was better than the marketing department's plan. Although his approach was a little off, and I knew it would not work, I allowed him to try it for a few months. I wanted him to learn from this experience.

As I checked in with him on his team's progress during those two months, it was clear to me that the strategy was not working. He finally recognized that his strategy was not effective.

This created a good coaching moment. So we had a productive discussion about his learnings from the experience. One of the lessons he said he absorbed was that he appreciated my allowing him to experiment without the fear of retaliation or punishment. He said he wanted to emulate this leadership behavior by being less directive himself and allowing his team to be more innovative.

For many leaders, failures come as a struggle. They are unsure if they should reprimand or coach. The rule of thumb is to coach unless the employee keeps making the same mistake and does not learn from failure.

If your people are not making mistakes, they are not learning or growing. New experiences create new learnings. New learnings, in turn, can lead to greater success. Conversely, if your team is successful, you must learn from the success. Ask your team, "What did we do well?" And "How can we use this learning to succeed in the future?" And "What adjustments do we need to make to be more successful in the future?"

It is also critical that leaders learn from their own adversity. When leaders share those learnings with their team members, it helps the employees to see that their leader acknowledges that she is not perfect.

Milton Goggans, a former senior vice president of Bristol-Myers Squibb, said, "Employees want to work for leaders that have experienced adversity." Employees will have confidence that the leader has gained experience, has learned from the challenges, and is capable of leading them through adversity.

Learn from Success

I remember leading a large sales team that had been unsuccessful for a number of years. They simply did not trust that their leader was out to help them. Therefore, there was little trust throughout the team.

I spent time getting to know the team and listening to their thoughts and ideas. I used every interaction to try to inspire them to be better. I made adjustments to the team's expectations and helped them develop a culture that both rewarded excellent coaching and recognized those who exceeded expectations.

THE PERFECT LEADERSHIP TRIAD

After about nine months, our team moved to the top position in the sales organization.

In a team meeting held about three months after they were consistently being ranked at the top, I asked my direct reports why we were successful. At first the team struggled to explain it. Finally, one leader remarked, "You convinced us that we could win if we followed a process." Others chimed in that we had developed a strong, coaching-centered focus. Some suggested that one factor was that they had learned to trust each other more.

The truth is that there were several things we did to succeed. I believe that our coaching-centered culture, paired with a focus on autonomy and development, was a huge difference maker. Focusing on people and coaching led to better performance.

How Effective Are You at Coaching?

Here are two questions to ask yourself as you consider your coaching effectiveness. In addition to asking yourself both questions, I would recommend that you ask your direct reports the second question. Then compare your perception versus their perception of your coaching.

How effective do you believe you are at coaching your direct reports?
  a) Very effective (top 20% of the company)
  b) Effective (top 50% of company)
  c) Somewhat ineffective (bottom 50% of company)
  d) Ineffective (you do not coach at all)

If you were to survey your direct reports, how effective would they say you are at coaching?

a) Very effective (top 20% of the company)

b) Effective (top 50% of company)

c) Somewhat ineffective (bottom 50% of company)

d) Ineffective (you do not coach at all)

In a recent survey of a Fortune 500 company, leaders ranked themselves in the 80th percentile for their coaching effectiveness. But when their direct reports were surveyed, they rated their leaders only in the 30th percentile. Obviously, there is a significant delta between the leaders' perception of their coaching and the opinion of their direct reports. (Scott Edinger, "Sales Teams Need More (and Better) Coaching," *Harvard Business Review,* May 8, 2015, https://hbr.org/2015/05/a-high-percentage-move-to-increase-revenue)

How does this happen? Leaders tend to believe that they are more effective at many skills than those around them believe. It is what I call the "missing mirror principle." Leaders simply do not look in the mirror to find the truth. Until a leader looks in the mirror, is honest with herself, and seeks input from the "friends of the mirror" (direct reports, peers, and supervisors), there will always be a disconnect between perception and reality.

Additionally, I believe that most leaders provide feedback and tell employees what to do, instead of coaching them. As we have seen, there is a significant difference between feedback, telling, and coaching. There is an appropriate time to tell and provide feedback, as noted in the section on situational coaching.

Just remember: your direct reports don't only want to know what they are doing right or wrong; they want to know how they can improve. This requires effective coaching. It is only when a leader learns how to effectively coach, and then coaches his direct reports, that he can help improve how employees think and act.

I have asked these same two questions of groups in a slightly different way. I have inquired how the leaders rate themselves at coaching. Then I have requested them to rate the effectiveness of their supervisors' coaching. Again, the leaders rate their own coaching effectiveness significantly higher than their bosses' coaching effectiveness.

As an executive, I supervised a leader who shared the story of her coaching and leadership effectiveness early in her career. After a year of ineffective coaching and leadership, which she recognized and acknowledged, she asked her team what she needed to do to improve. It takes a confident and authentic leader to ask a question like this when you know you have been ineffective.

The response from her team was candid. They provided numerous examples of ineffective leadership and made suggestions on what she could do differently. She listened to their advice and feedback. And she made changes. As a result, she became a better coach and leader because she listened and was coachable.

Fast forward about eight years. She was promoted to an executive position. Her desire to improve and her honesty with herself and her team helped her to become a better coach and leader.

Question-Centered Problem Solving

Thinking takes place as silent, internal questions and answers. That is why coaching requires the ability to ask great questions to encourage deeper thinking. Effective coaches avoid giving advice. Instead, they ask questions that help employees find their own best answer! Their best answers become their own best advice.

Great coaches ask inspiring, catalytic questions. When an employee asks you what to do, ask them what she thinks will work for the situation. Then ask her for alternative solutions. Allow the employee to develop and act on her self-identified best solution, thereby empowering her to make future decisions.

In 1943, Edwin Land's granddaughter asked him why she couldn't see the photograph he had taken right then. The result of his granddaughter's catalytic question was the Polaroid camera that Land developed and commercialized a few years later.

It has been said that all the answers are out there. All we have to do is ask the right question. Usually the right question leads to the right answer. The best way to solve a problem, then, is to develop better questions.

I have taken many groups through a question-centered, problem-solving exercise. The premise of the exercise is to discover the right question to answer before ever seeking a solution.

The exercise works like this: first, I state a rule that for the first five minutes no one can ask a clarifying question about a participant's question or make a statement. The only thing participants are allowed to do is ask a question about the problem we are trying to solve.

It is very tempting for participants to comment or make statements, but as the exercise continues, you can see the lightbulbs start to come on. They begin to develop deep, meaningful questions that get to the heart of the issue. Usually within three to five minutes, we have discovered the *real* question that needs to be answered.

Once the right question is identified, it is significantly easier to find the best solution. I would encourage you to use this exercise with your team. Too often we spend our time finding the answer to the wrong question. Identify the best question *before* you seek a solution.

Let me illustrate. I once led a group of leaders through this exercise in a large organization. Their organization was struggling with how important a certain department in their business was to the company.

I started out by asking them, "What is the question you are trying to solve?" The immediate response was, "Should we dissolve this department?"

I asked them to step back for a moment to consider other questions that could be asked. At this point, I explained the process we were going to follow. I let them know that for the next five minutes, all they could do is ask a question about the challenge and no one could make comments about the questions raised.

The group struggled for the first couple of minutes. Every time someone raised a question, another person would chime in with a comment. I stopped the group to remind them of the rules: no comments, just questions.

What happened next was amazing. Within a few minutes, better questions emerged.... "What short-term and long-term value does this department bring to the organization?" "Has the department received the appropriate support it needs to be successful?" "Are the right leaders in place, and are they set up for success?" The questions continued to pour out as the leaders considered many questions that needed to be asked.

Eventually, the group uncovered the right question that needed to be asked. Then answers could be found. The result was a decision that considered all the alternatives and was right for the organization.

Again, before you solve a challenge or opportunity, make sure you uncover the right question that needs to be asked. Too many times, leaders answer the wrong question, or at least a less effective one.

The 80/20 Rule of Asking Questions and Coaching

Every question expands our range of possibilities. Each and every question gets us closer to the *best* question. As you seek the right solution, remember the 80/20 rule of leadership communication: you should spend 80 percent of the time asking questions about the question and 20 percent of the time coaching your employee to find the solution (or solutions).

So, how does this play out? As I have illustrated in the question-centered, problem-solving exercise, the leader should spend most of the time helping the employee find the right question to answer. This is the bulk of the solution process. When the leader and the employee both feel comfortable, they have found the right question to answer. They can then focus the last 20 percent of the time on discovering the solution.

In one organization, I worked with a second-line leader who was struggling with believing my observation that he needed to coach more effectively. His belief was that he was already a solid coach. So I conducted a live coaching session where I observed him coach one of his direct reports.

What I discovered was quite different than his own estimation of himself. He was really a below-average coach. As we debriefed about the coaching session, he resisted my feedback and coaching. He knew he needed to improve his own coaching skills, but still felt that he was above average. As a result, I stepped back and took him through the question-centered, problem-solving process to see if we could find a question that better addressed the situation.

While he struggled at first to find a question to ask, he eventually came up with some really good ones, like these: "What is the worst thing that could happen if I became a better coach?" And "What is the best thing that can happen?" And "What impact would my better coaching have on my team and their individual performance?"

We spent significant time asking questions before ever trying to find the best solution. Once he found the right question, he was able to recognize how improving as a coach could affect his team while at the same time heightening his leadership competencies.

Five Types of Great Coaching Questions

What are some great coaching questions that you can immediately implement as a leader? Here are five types of questions, with examples for each one:

» Insight Generation
  • Are you open to suggestions?
  • What is your perspective on...?
  • What has to happen in order for you to feel...?
» Understanding Purpose and Motivation
  • What part of the job gives you the greatest sense of purpose?
  • I recognize that many things may motivate you. What are your top three motivators?
  • The One Thing my manager can do to inspire me is...?
» Leadership/Coaching-focused
  • How do you like to be coached?

71

- What can I do to support you?
- What would *you* do if you were the leader of this team?
  » Team-focused
    - What will you contribute to our team?
    - What are your strengths as a team member?
    - What training is needed for this team?
    - What should our team accomplish?
  » Work-focused
    - What is your burning ambition for this year?
    - What are you going to do differently this year?
    - What are your three biggest challenges?
    - What are your three greatest opportunities?

More-Powerful Coaching Questions

Below are powerful questions to ask your employees. I promise that you will be surprised at some of the responses you will hear! Ask and then listen intently.

1. Where are we going as an organization?

2. Where are *you* going?

3. What is going well?

4. How can I help?

5. What suggestions do you have for the organization or even for me?

6. Are you open to suggestions?

7. If you were the coach for yourself, what advice would you have for you? (This is "feed-forward" instead of "feedback.")

8. What would you do if you were the leader of this team?

I have gleaned key insights about employees' attitudes, perceptions, needs, and feelings by asking these questions. The answers to them provide a window into the thinking process of your employees, which will greatly assist your coaching.

You do not need to ask all these questions during a single meeting. I would recommend, instead, that you ask them over a period of several weeks or even months, depending on the frequency of your meetings with your employees.

Failure to Coach and Develop Senior Leaders

As I mentioned at the beginning of the book, many senior executives feel that they do not have the time to develop their direct reports—or even themselves. In fact, many senior leaders consciously choose *not* to coach their vice presidents and instead contract that out to executive coaches. While this is a reality, it is a mistake.

My experience is that senior leaders, especially senior vice presidents and above, are expected to know how to do their jobs and do not need much development. As we have seen, however, everyone needs a coach so they can develop and become more effective.

My advice to senior leaders, then, is to consciously coach and develop your leaders. Emulate what great coaching looks like. Show your leaders how important coaching is in the organization.

Equally important, a senior leader should seek out coaching for herself. So ask your own supervisor for coaching. It is not a sign of weakness. Share with your supervisor how you like to be coached.

Every leader has a boss—and every leader needs coaching.

Conclusion

If coaching drives performance and productivity, why do so few leaders do it? I believe that most leaders simply do not know the difference between coaching and providing feedback or direction.

Most leaders seem more comfortable with telling employees what and how to do things. That requires less time than asking the employee probing questions to help them solve their own challenges. Many leaders think this is the same thing as coaching. As we have seen, however, coaching is very different from merely telling or providing feedback. Coaching is question-centered and inquiry-driven.

When leaders learn to coach effectively, they open the door to success. They grow and develop their people. They demonstrate that they care about and trust their people. Leaders who take the time to coach develop followers. They build mutual trust and respect. They create and enhance strong, high-performing teams. They maximize productivity, increase profits, and drive revenue!

Ask yourself these questions about coaching-centered leadership:

» What are the differences between coaching, telling, and providing feedback?

» As you think about your last employee who left the organization, did you do everything you could to coach, teach, and develop him?

» How will you know when to tell, provide feedback, or coach an employee?

» How can you use peer coaching to develop your people?

» What can you do to give your people the autonomy to do their job in the manner they want to?

» How can you better learn from failures and successes?

» When will you ask your direct reports how effective you are at coaching?

» What can you do to be more effective at asking your people catalytic coaching questions that will help them think better?

4

Coaching Culture

> *"The only thing of real importance that leaders do is to create and change culture."*
>
> –**Edgar Schein**

Coaching Culture

A people-focused and performance-driven culture starts with coaching. A coaching culture is established by focusing your leaders on how to ask their employees catalytic questions, to listen so that they open up a creative process, to partner with and assist employees to develop solutions to opportunities as well as challenges, and to help employees become more productive and effective.

Organizations with strong coaching cultures have developed a clear definition of coaching. One common definition used by organizations comes from the International Coaching Federation (ICF). It defines coaching as "partnering with clients in a thought-provoking and creative process that inspires them to maximize their personal and professional potential." In other words, helping your employees think better will help them be more productive.

The ICF has defined a coaching culture as an organization that has at least five of the following six elements:

1. Employees value coaching.

2. Senior executives value coaching.

3. The organization includes internal and external coaches and leaders who use coaching skills.

4. Leaders and coaches receive accredited, coach-specific training.

5. Coaching is a line item in the budget.

6. All employees have equal access to either internal or external coaching.

The ICF, in conjunction with the Human Capital Institute, found that organizations that have at least five of these elements are at minimum 61 percent more likely to have improved talent outcomes. These outcomes include better employee engagement, more internal promotions, increased shareholder value, higher profitability, and greater customer satisfaction. (https://coachfederation.org/research/building-a-coaching-culture)

Developing a Coaching Culture

At Texas Tech University Health Sciences Center, the human resource organization led by Steve Sosland, its chief people officer, developed a coaching culture. Using the ICF definition of coaching, ICF coaching principles, and the six elements of a coaching organization, it hired both accredited and credentialed internal and external coaches. Senior leaders then supported and modeled the resulting coaching. Leaders at every level had either an internal or an external coach.

The principle of "leader as coach" was established throughout the organization, with all leaders learning how to coach effectively. Leaders were evaluated on coaching effectiveness. The result has been a culture of accountability where coaches are responsible for coaching and employees are expected to be coachable.

In 2019, TTUHSC was voted, for the first time, one of the top 100 universities to work for. In fact, the number one reason now given by new employees for joining the organization is its culture.

You can start developing a coaching culture by teaching senior leaders what coaching is and what it is not. Senior leaders need to learn how to ask more effective questions, to listen to and encourage employees to reflect, and to develop insights and perspective before taking action on an opportunity. They should start asking questions to help individuals gain more insight on what—and why—something happened. Leaders should ask the employee how she would handle it the next time, instead of just telling her what to do.

Senior leaders are bought into the coaching culture, model it, and live it. Every company culture starts with senior leadership. If someone on the senior leadership team is not all in or does not support a coaching culture, that is addressed. Senior leaders are vocal about the importance of coaching and recognize leaders who are proven to be coaching effectively.

You are well advised to invest in coaching for your entire management team. I would recommend external credentialed executive coaches for the C-suite, vice presidents, and directors. An external credentialed coach can energize the leaders and help them understand the overall value of coaching.

Many successful organizations strengthen their coaching cultures by using internal coaches to complement external coaches. It is important that internal coaches attend accredited coaching schools and become credentialed through the International Coaching Federation. As an organization promotes employees to internal coaching positions, it should understand that the credibility of the coaches will be influenced by their reputations in their previous roles.

Organizations will want to ensure that senior managers are being effectively trained and coached. This can be accomplished through coach-the-coach training sessions, along with workshops. You might also consider having key senior leaders and directors attend formal coach training for certification. While this requires a longer-term commitment, these leaders will become well-versed in coaching methods and will become allies for the culture. When leaders truly believe in and support a coaching culture, they will become strong advocates and voices for that culture.

It is vital to create a structured process with clear goals. You will want to create and allow the time for coaching. Time should be set aside for coaching discussions. One step you can take immediately is to allocate at least 30 minutes of coaching for each employee every week. I practiced this at previous companies and found that my employees, through my example and modeling of how to coach, learned first-hand how to effectively coach their own employees.

Coaching becomes ingrained in the DNA of every leader. It is important to provide feedback when a leader is not following the process or supporting the coaching culture.

You provide the financial and educational resources to ensure success. Funds are set aside in a coaching budget with a separate line item.

"Coaching the coach" includes recognizing and rewarding effective coaches. In one organization, I established a Coach of the Year award to recognize the top coaches. The award included all leaders down to first-line managers.

This award set the tone for how serious I was about coaching. First-line managers and directors recognized that if they could improve and become more effective coaches, they would be recognized and rewarded. That created an opportunity to reinforce the importance of effective coaching and also helped ingrain it into the DNA of my organization.

Finally, leaders are evaluated frequently to measure their coaching skills. While I suggest frequent evaluations, they should at a minimum occur during both midyear and annual reviews.

Seven Coaching Core Competencies

When evaluating the coaching competencies of your leaders, especially during reviews, here are seven that are aligned with the ICF Competency Model. A leader:

1. Develops trust with each employee

2. Candidly communicates with employees

3. Actively listens to employees

4. Is open to other peoples' perspectives, especially those of direct reports

5. Identifies and understands the immediate and future coaching needs of each employee

6. Asks powerful, catalytic questions when coaching employees

7. Holds each employee accountable for their performance

When leaders are held accountable for basic coaching competencies, they will better understand the expectations and be more likely to improve their coaching.

Novo Nordisk: Coaching-Centered Leadership Culture

At Novo Nordisk, senior leaders under the direction of Lars Rebien Sørensen, the former CEO, developed formal coaching programs for senior executives. In the United States, Andy Ajello, former senior vice president of Diabetes and Obesity Sales, set out to develop a coaching culture within the sales force. He started by engaging his own external executive coach. He asked each of his direct reports and second-line leaders to engage an external executive coach. This reinforced the importance he sought to establish of coaching within the organization. Some leaders took an additional step and sought out professional executive coaching certifications.

Ajello set the expectation that each first-line leader would have 120 annual coaching days with their direct reports. Coaching days were documented for both first- and second-line leaders.

Ajello used quarterly Plan of Action meetings to conduct coaching clinics to "fire up the coaches and the leadership teams" and to help them become better coaches. Each first-line manager was allowed to pick the specific coaching curriculum that they wanted to follow, based on their needs. This ongoing process developed leaders who could effectively coach.

Elements of a Coaching-Centered Leadership Culture

A culture of learning and coaching is vital for the development of employees. To implement a coaching culture, a process is developed to ensure effective coaching as the leader training proceeds. The Leader Coach should represent the mantra of the organization. I will speak more about this in the next chapter.

As mentioned previously, it is important to recognize that this all starts with buy-in by senior leadership. It requires both the modeling of a coaching culture by senior leaders and a financial commitment.

Coaching can bring about a more empowering, inclusive, and innovative culture in which the employees' strengths and talents can be leveraged, and in which employees own and are responsible for their development and performance.

Organizations adopting a coaching-centered culture typically take pains to create a well-organized and well-structured learning and talent development program. Coaching is integrated into their overall talent management strategy. The collective efforts of the training department, the talent management group, human resources, and a senior leader sponsor can ensure that this happens.

Training simply cannot be a one-time event. Effective training focuses on developing the leadership team over time. It is a consistent process with ongoing coaching, follow-up, and accountability. It is important to recognize at the start that developmental opportunities are more important than merely training.

Studies show that the most effective training is experiential. It is on-the-job experiences that stretch and challenge employees at all levels. Employees who are given opportunities to develop and learn new things will be more engaged, and productivity and retention will increase.

BASF Canada Coaching-Centered Leadership Culture

Several companies have established effective coaching-centered cultures. One business that has done this particularly well is BASF Canada's Crop Protection division, a group that develops and manufactures crop protection products for Canadian farmers:

> Thirteen years ago, BASF Canada started their Managerial Coaching program. Managers complete a one-year program that includes monthly coaching sessions with an external coach. The coaching conversations often focus on how managers can coach their direct reports to succeed in their role. At the beginning and the end of the program, managers engage in a 360 [degree] process to provide them with valuable feedback and track improvement over the course of the program. This program is only one example of how BASF Canada is committed to promoting a coaching culture.

> Ron Kehler, the Business Director of BASF Canada–Crop Protection, was asked why creating a coaching culture at BASF was so important. "A coaching culture means continuous feedback and improvement in employee development," he said. "Providing coaching to people managers along with training people managers on how to coach

their teams creates a consistent feedback loop for employees that accelerates their development."

Ron noted that as a result of the program he has seen more self-awareness among his employees, stronger employee-manager working relationships, and increased openness to constructive feedback beyond from just their direct manager. ("How to Create a Coaching Culture in Your Company," Leann Schneider and Tim Jackson, Special to the *Globe and Mail,* May 16, 2018)

Lead through Coaching, Not Just by Walking Around

Much has been said over the years about "leadership by walking around." The focus of this principle is about listening to, learning from, and communicating with employees. While this is effective, the truth is that greater leadership impact comes through effectively coaching everyone in the organization. Implicit in coaching is the unified concept of listening, learning, teaching, and helping people think more effectively about the business.

In my experience in several organizations, I followed a simple rule of *Go, Look, See, and Do,* which I believe combines the benefits of walking around *and* coaching.

Go suggests taking action by getting out from behind your desk. Leadership takes place in the trenches, not solely in the boardroom. If a leader is to understand the opportunities and challenges in the marketplace, he should get out to *Look* and *See* what the employees and customers are experiencing.

Look means that you use your eyes to observe what is happening. Are employees engaged and passionate? Are the customers' needs being met by the organization? What challenges are the employees experiencing?

See means the leader not only observes with her eyes but uses her intellect and curiosity to comprehend the meaning of every situation. This provides insights to the leader, so she knows how to coach the employee.

Behind the *Do* rule is a need to consistently coach each employee to be more effective. Whether that means being more effective with the customer, or in her role, or in a specific situation, *Do* is all about actively coaching the employee to grow and develop.

Our Inner Voice

An external coaching voice can challenge and encourage our inner voice. We all hear the voice inside our head. Usually, however, the voice limits us and impedes us from achieving our goals.

I have spoken to many leaders and future leaders about this limiting voice we all hear and listen to. I remember the first time I was promoted to an executive position. I heard the voice. It told me I wasn't prepared to do the job. I began to think,

"What am I going to do when they figure out that I cannot do this job and that there are other people more qualified?"

In reality, I *knew* I could do the job and I had spent many years preparing for it. Yet the voice tried to limit my belief that I was competent. This is where outside coaching can help.

The one thing I have learned is that if you want to get better at something, it's difficult to do it alone. If we allow a qualified outsider—in this case, a credentialed coach—to put his eyes on the limiting beliefs, we can often see new possibilities. As both an executive *and* a credentialed coach, I have always used a trained, external coach. These coaches have given me new perspectives and challenged me to think differently.

So, if you want to accelerate your career, strengthen your business acumen, and increase your productivity and performance, then consider getting a coach. Do your due diligence and find someone who has achieved excellence and success, and then see if she will be a good fit. Find someone you can trust and then ask her to push you and challenge you to become a better leader.

Coaching: A Change Process

When leaders coach, they are implementing a change process that follows the traditional change innovation curve, as shown in figure 1. Change happens more quickly in a coaching culture. Leaders accelerate change when they use coaching. Coaching, in turn, leads to an agile culture because it helps employees plan and execute change better and faster.

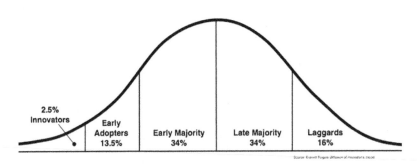

Figure 1: Everett Roger's Diffusion of Innovation Curve

As Roger's Diffusion of Innovation Curve depicts, with effective coaching, you will grow leaders and employees who will be innovators and early adopters. These are the creators and visionaries for your company who will ultimately boost its success. These are the leaders who should be used to promote and lead your coaching culture.

Once you have these people onboard, you move to the early majority (also called the pragmatists). They will make decisions based on their intellect and minds. Once the early majority are aboard, it will be much easier to get the conservative late majority. My suggestion would be to leave the laggards alone. They may never truly believe in your coaching culture and probably should not even be in the organization.

Understanding the Roger's Curve is vitally important for leaders. They are the ones who will focus on early wins to convert employees to the coaching culture and move their way through the innovation curve, realizing that not everyone will buy into or even understand the importance of a coaching culture. Remember, change is individualized and occurs one person at a time.

When it comes to actual coaching, leaders need to understand that behavioral, developmental, and performance changes will follow the Roger's Curve.

As depicted in figure 2, an effective process is available to create change.

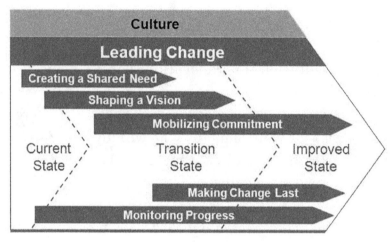

Figure 2: Steps to make change

At the heart of coaching is having an employee who is coachable. Those people who are generally coachable are that way because they feel a need to improve. Even when their people are coachable, leaders should be prepared to help create cognitive dissonance with employees they are coaching to help instill in them a healthy sense of urgency to improve. When employees and leaders come together with a shared need to improve so that they can move the business forward, the coaching change process truly begins.

It is critical that leaders first hold a strong vision of what coaching is and how it will help get employees—and the organization—to the next level of development. Leaders frequently communicate that vision through metaphors and inspiring success stories.

The leader's next responsibility is to mobilize the commitment of his team to both desire and accept coaching. Inspiring and mobilizing the team is arguably the most important responsibility a leader is given. A leader recognizes each team member's key motivators and regularly appeals to those motivators to move the employee toward change.

Leaders are ultimately responsible for making the coaching change stick. Consistent and frequent coaching is the foundation. As you move up the funnel of coaching, you end with action on the part of the employee. This is where accountability and progress are measured. This is where change becomes measurable.

Barriers to Establishing a Coaching Culture

The most significant barrier to developing a coaching culture is a lack of leadership from senior executives. If senior leaders talk about coaching but do not model it, they are sending a message throughout the organization that coaching is not a priority.

Additionally, if senior leaders consistently tell their direct reports what to do, other leaders will follow their lead. Instead of a coaching culture, companies end up with a telling culture. Senior leaders lead through example by modeling good coaching. They should share coaching successes with employees at every opportunity.

If coaching is to become part of the organizational DNA, the senior leadership team sets the expectation that every leader should therefore be a strong coach. Most important, leaders at every level are trained to become effective coaches.

Many organizations and leaders lack a full understanding of what coaching actually is. Therefore, the organization needs to develop a definition of coaching that all employees, especially leaders, understand.

Leaders recognize that every touch point with an employee is an opportunity to inspire and coach. When leaders are not intentional with employee conversations, employees will not have the necessary reinforcement of coaching's importance.

Another obstacle is when leaders do not understand the value of coaching. As we saw in chapter 3, the consulting giant Deloitte has proven that companies having strong coaching cultures are more productive and maximize profit. These organizations also attract and retain key talent.

If a strong coaching culture is to be developed, it requires that companies develop coaching as a key competency. Therefore, leaders at every level are provided coach training. Coach-the-coach programs are operationalized by the human resources, talent management, and training departments. Coaching tools and resources are provided to leaders at every level. Most likely, external executive coaches will need to be hired to do this training and also to coach senior executives.

Lack of time to practice coaching as well as issues of funding and commitment are serious barriers. As with any skill, if leaders do not commit to the time required to be trained and then to practice coaching, that skill will never be fully developed. So senior leaders will want to set an expectation that coaches spend time coaching their direct reports, especially during one-on-one meetings.

Lack of recognition is another barrier. It is advisable that leaders are recognized and rewarded for effective coaching. This can be measured by actual results, the development of coaching skills, engagement, and retention of employees, among other indicators. Coach of the Year awards and other recognition can be used.

Start with Your Team

What do you do, though, if your organization does not have a coaching culture? Start building your own with your team! You do not need to be a credentialed coach to do this. You only need to have the desire to coach, learn, and develop the coaching competencies, and then to spend sufficient time coaching your employees.

As you do this, you will find that trust will grow within your team, engagement will increase as employees recognize that you really care about them and want them to improve, and their performance will increase over time.

Another benefit to developing a coaching culture within your team is that your boss and *her* boss will see the difference that your coaching is making. This could lead to an organization-wide emphasis on coaching.

Conclusion

Coaching is the glue that holds a culture together. Coaching maximizes the performance of the organization, while increasing engagement and retention. One of the paradoxes of coaching is that it requires engaged employees, though engagement naturally occurs and even increases with effective coaching.

Coaching is more effective than training alone, because it is an ongoing and continuous process, not just a one-time event. The success of coaching, therefore, is predicated on the commitment of the organization and its leaders.

Coaching will bring about a more empowering and innovative culture where the employees' strengths and talents can be leveraged, and where employees will own their performance.

Remember, one of the top reasons people leave their job is the lack of developmental opportunities. Coaching helps identify growth opportunities for employees and helps them develop their competencies and skills. A culture of learning and coaching is vital for the development of employees, every bit as much as it is for the organization's bottom line.

Organizations do not create sustainable coaching cultures alone. People do. It is through each leader's actions, attitudes, and behaviors that a coaching culture is created and sustained. It is created by leaders and employees who want to be coached so that they can improve.

Finally, a coaching culture provides a sustainable competitive advantage—especially since few organizations have been successful at implementing one! If your organization can create and build a coaching culture, you will be more profitable, ensure engagement with employees, and retain key talent. Your culture will be inimitable.

As we will see in the next chapter, having engaged Leader Coaches will be the lifeblood of the organization.

Ask yourself these questions about your coaching culture:

» What is my organization's definition of coaching?

» How would I describe the current coaching culture of my team and the overall organization?

» Which elements of the six defined requirements of a coaching culture do you currently have in your organization?

» How many of the seven coaching core competencies do I possess? What am I doing to develop all seven of them?

» What steps do I need to take to create or build a coaching culture?

» Do I know who on my team is more open to change and who is less or even not open to change?

» What are the obstacles, for my team and organization, to implement a coaching culture?

5

Leader Coach

"Coaching is something we do with people, not to people."

–**Ken Blanchard**, *noted business book writer*

Coaching is the sine qua non of leadership. Understanding how each employee wants to be coached is vital for the success of a leader. Implicit in seeking this understanding is an acknowledgment that the leader cares about her people. Coaching provides an excellent opportunity to build trust.

An effective Leader Coach partners with employees to help them think creatively so they can solve business challenges and exploit opportunities. A Leader Coach teaches and coaches each employee to think effectively even when the coach is not there. This engenders confidence in the employee's ability.

A Leader Coach reinforces that the employee owns the outcome and has the autonomy to complete the task as she wishes. The Leader Coach holds the employee accountable for the actions she has committed to complete as well as for the outcome.

What a Leader Coach Looks Like

> *"Before you are a leader, success is all about growing yourself. When you become a leader, success is all about growing others."*
>
> –**Jack Welch**, *former CEO, General Electric*

When I was an executive, I once supervised a leader who epitomized the qualities of a Leader Coach. He was not only a great coach; he was a terrific role model. Every interaction he had with his direct reports involved developing his people into more effective employees. Time and again, he found or created developmental opportunities for his people.

His people skills, which we sometimes refer to as soft skills, were outstanding. He understood how his people thought. He knew not only what to do but how to do it effectively. This is the type of executive every leader should want on her team.

An effective Leader Coach adheres to the principles of great coaching. She models coaching in everything she does. Her focus is on building competencies and trust through coaching. A strong Leader Coach understands that she is being paid on how her team performs, and not as much on her personal performance. Whenever a leader fails to coach effectively, she is losing an opportunity to help her people develop and grow the business.

A Leader Coach tailors coaching to the strengths, weaknesses, and needs of each individual. Additionally, they align their coaching with the needs of the organization. In fact, an effective

Leader Coach understands the core competencies that the company has outlined for each position so that she can coach every employee to acquire these competencies.

Importantly, a Leader Coach also spends time with employees on career development. She is accountable for the development of her people, while the employee is responsible to develop himself. A Leader Coach creates opportunities for employees to develop their skills, provides resources, and holds productive conversations about their growth and development. In sum, she is a proactive supporter of individual development.

A Leader Coach knows the importance of her soft skills. She recognizes that while she may understand the overall purpose of the business and what to do, how she does things in her leadership role is what has the greatest influence on her employees.

I had a strategy professor in graduate school who shared his experience as a consultant at Bain & Company, a prestigious consulting firm. He once shared with me the difference between good and great consultants.

He taught that the baseline to perform as a consultant was to listen to the client. The good consultants would then execute on the strategy and plan. But the *great* consultants added a third dimension: they added value to the client and to the firm.

Now, think of this in terms of a Leader Coach. The baseline of being such a leader is to learn to really listen to the employee. That Leader Coach can then ask effective questions to help the employee execute on the corporate strategic plan, as well as their individual job responsibilities. The great Leader Coach adds one important element: She has the ability to add value to the employee by asking catalytic questions, helping the employee think through smarter solutions, and holding the employee accountable to execute on solutions that add value to the customers and the company.

Humility: A Key Trait of a Leader Coach

Humility leads to trust. And trust is the foundation of all relationships. Employees need to know that a leader is trustworthy and will do what she says she is going to do. Leaders endear themselves to employees when they are both transparent and honest.

Leadership at Novo Nordisk exemplified this principle of humility. Göran Ando, M.D., former chairman of the company's board, stated, "Leadership at Novo Nordisk is humble. The chances that your people will respect and follow you are infinitely higher if you are a good, true, humble human being."

He went on to say, "Novo Nordisk will never have corporate planes. Not that they cannot afford planes but because of the message it would send to the organization." This is an example of humility in action.

Lars Rebien Sørensen, a former CEO of the same company, and a two-time winner of Harvard's "Best Performing CEO in the World" honor, is a great example of humility. From my observations of him, he takes responsibility for setbacks and defers all credit for successes to his people.

Humble, successful leaders almost always attribute their success to the people they surround themselves with. They trust their people and give them autonomy to do their job. Most important, humble leaders listen to employees, thereby building mutual trust with them.

While others may assume that these leaders are extraordinarily smart, in fact a humble leader recognizes that she does not have all the answers. She realizes that she is likely surrounded by people smarter than she. So she is willing to learn from others. She will even say, "I am sorry" when necessary—something many leaders fail to do, thinking that's somehow beneath them.

Be Yourself!

"Becoming a leader is synonymous with becoming yourself. It is precisely that simple and it is also that difficult."

–**Warren Bennis**, *world-renowned leader in leadership studies*

Do you ever feel that those who are around you are judging you even when you yourself feel you are being really authentic? If that happens, are you comfortable enough to still be yourself?

I was recently coaching an author, thought leader, and entrepreneur who is truly an authentic leader. She shared with me her struggles and fears with sometimes feeling judged when she opened up and explored her vulnerabilities with her followers and consults.

As we explored her feelings about being judged, she explained that her husband and children are not judgmental. She even shared with me examples of her online posts and blogs in which she was candid and authentic about her personal leadership and life challenges. What I found most amazing was that the responses to her posts were completely positive while her posts were always appreciated by her followers.

What was even more amazing was that as we explored her struggle with feeling that she was often being negatively judged, she could only think of one person in her life who was judgmental of her—her mother. As we explored that particular situation, it became evident that while she longed for her mother's support she felt only judgment.

One person out of thousands was making her feel judged, and as a result she was transferring that feeling of being judged to all her followers. When she thought of it that way, it became truly eye opening to her. So she decided that she was *not* going to let one person change her core-being and authentic approach to her life and business. She decided to let her voice be heard!

If you yourself have feelings that people are judging you, I would encourage you to explore whether this is reality or instead self-doubt and concern for something that is not reality-based. As we watch and read the many posts on social media, think about some of the many books specific to our field that we have digested, and reflect on the dozens of workshops that we have attended, I think most of us would agree that candor and authenticity endear us to other people. We feel comfortable knowing that they have the same challenges that we have.

In one company, I supervised a leader who shared his failures, challenges, and learnings with his team. His appropriate self-disclosure really endeared him to his team. So whenever he asked his team for something, they knew he was completely on their team, and as a result they trusted him. They believed that he would not ask anything of them that he wouldn't do himself.

This type of honesty and candor is contagious. The more honest you are with your team, the more candid they will be with you. Just like the old saying "You reap what you sow," what you put into something is what you get back. Trust in, trust out. Candor in, candor out. Coaching in, trust out. This should be the goal of every leader.

We have all had life experiences that have shaped us. We each have met many challenges in our lifetime. I remember one leader essentially saying, "Treat everyone you meet as if they have serious problems, and you will be right most of the time." If these things are true, and I believe they are, why should we let someone keep us from being authentic and real? If there is one leadership lesson that I have learned in my career, it is *Be Yourself!*

Benefits of a Leader Coach

> *"Leadership is about making others better as a result of your presence and making sure that impact lasts in your absence."*
>
> –**Sheryl Sandberg**, *COO of Facebook*

When a leader coaches his team, he demonstrates that he cares about them. He builds trust, because effective coaching requires honesty and candor from both coaching participants. Leaders who consistently coach will soon garner real respect from their team members.

Likewise, the employee feels respected. The leader has an opportunity to demonstrate his competencies and listening skills. Remember that when people know you care about and respect them, they will buy into your vision and work even harder for you.

Leaders who coach effectively learn to listen. Listening, in turn, leads to better solutions. When a leader opens up and listens to others' perspectives, that builds trust. They demonstrate that they themselves can be influenced, and that others can participate in the decision-making process.

Coaching requires the leader to be more open to suggestions and ideas. This will help the leader as much as the employee. Great Leader Coaches learn to execute on the ideas developed by their team.

It is critical that your team knows your expectations and your vision. You will want to communicate these clearly and often.

One of the top reasons for coaching is that it will give you insights into the thinking process of your team members. By listening to them during coaching sessions, you can tell if they understand and buy into your vision. You will know if they understand your expectations. Coaching is a lens into the minds of your people.

I will never forget one executive whom I led. He was candid and open with his team. He did not tell them how to do things, but gave them autonomy. He listened to them and asked for input on decisions that he needed to make. He not only listened, he often acted on their ideas. This attitude created a bond of trust with his entire team.

He coached them consistently and effectively. He genuinely cared about the development of his people, and it showed. He also cared about their performance. When an employee was not performing well, he had the managerial courage to address the low performance. As a result, his team's performance was consistently high. He was a great Leader Coach.

When you coach people to grow, develop, and improve, you become a more effective leader. The act of helping others benefits you. This principle is one of the paradoxes of leadership. The trust grows within your team, performance improves, and employee retention increases.

As Galileo Galilei said, "One cannot teach a man anything. One can only enable him to learn from within himself." The best way to do this is by being a Leader Coach.

Leader Coach as a Mentor

Establishing a mentoring relationship is vital for the success of new and experienced employees alike. Senior and mid-level executives regularly set aside time to mentor. That should always be part of the coaching culture. When leaders share their wisdom and experience, employees not only learn but also feel more connected to the company and its leadership.

It is important to understand the role of a mentor. A mentor is an experienced leader who spends time to support, provide guidance, share her perspective, and help develop an employee through a relationship-centered approach. Here are a few things a mentor should do:

» Share experiences and wisdom.

» Support the employee to set and achieve goals.

» Help the employee perform his job more effectively.

» Help the employee with his career progress and development.

» Assist the employee to navigate the politics of the organization, especially the colleagues he needs to develop a relationship with to achieve his goals.

» Help the employee understand his current role better.

» Encourage the employee to be accountable and own his personal learning and development.

According to Göran Ando, M.D., former board chair at Novo Nordisk, and cited earlier, executive leadership at Novo Nordisk has a structured mentoring and coaching program. Executive vice presidents, for example, are assigned to mentor high-potential executives, usually from another senior executive's division, to help them grow and develop and eventually to acquire a richer perspective on their roles and goals.

Ando emphasized that "There is structure to this mentoring and coaching. Most importantly, there is careful follow-up to the coaching."

Benefits of Mentoring for New Employees

Mentoring is especially important for new employees. They come into a company uncertain of the company culture, the expectations, and the leadership style of their new boss.

When Leader Coaches assign a mentor to a new employee, it ensures that the employee gets off to a quick start. The mentor can help the new employee clearly understand the role.

Mentor-based onboarding helps the employee gain a connection with her peers and staff. This results in higher engagement for the new employee *and* her staff.

The mentor can help the manager determine if the employee is a cultural fit. If it turns out that she does not fit the culture, action should be taken immediately. Mentors are a second set of eyes that can see where the new employee is strong and where she needs coaching and development. As Ando told me, "Organizations are smart. They will see performance before the leader does." In this case, the mentor will observe the true performance, probably before the leader does.

Mentor-based onboarding helps reduce costly turnover, primarily because the mentor can help the new employee feel connected to the company. Employees who have a mentor will be happier and more engaged. The result is a new Leader Coach who creates and maintains happy employees. Remember: happy employees improve the corporate bottom line.

"How I Want to Be Coached"—Two Questions

It simply amazes me when I consider the proportion of leaders who really have zero idea how individuals on their team desire to be coached. This is a huge miss by those leaders. Since understanding how your people want to be coached is vital for a leader's success, here are two multiple-choice questions to ask yourself:

1. Does my boss know how I like to be coached?
    a. I have communicated clearly to her how I like to be coached.
    b. I communicate to her during coaching sessions how I like to be coached.
    c. I have not communicated to her how I like to be coached.
    d. My boss does not coach me.

2. Do I know how my direct reports like to be coached?
   a. I have asked each of my direct reports how they liked to be coached.
   b. I have asked some of my direct reports how they like to be coached.
   c. I think I already know how they liked to be coached so I do not need to ask them.
   d. I have never asked my direct reports how they want to be coached.

Your answers to these two questions should provide guidance on what your next step should be. My experience is that it is rare for a leader to communicate to her boss how she wants to be coached or even to know how each of her direct reports likes to be coached. It is even more rare for employees to share with their supervisors how they want to be coached.

As a new leader in one organization, early in my career, it never dawned on me that I should ask employees how they wanted to be coached! Instead, like most leaders of the time, I assumed I was supposed to just figure it out, based on my knowledge of the employee and how he responded to my coaching. I soon found that this does not work.

I once had an executive whom I coached who was really struggling with his team. His people were simply not responding to his coaching. My first question was, "Have you asked them how they want to be coached?" His response was typical of most leaders of whom I ask this question: "I hadn't thought of that!" Or, more commonly, to save face an executive will respond, "I think I already *know* how they want to be coached. I have been working with them for a long time!"

While I was coaching another executive, he shared with me that an employee was not happy with the way she was being coached by him. As he listened to her, it was clear that the issue wasn't poor coaching. Rather, he was not appealing to her motivators and needs.

After a conversation with me, he went back to the employee and had her complete the How I Want to Be Coached Tool, given below. When he reviewed her responses, he felt really shocked by her needs and wants when it came to coaching. He soon course-corrected, and the coaching relationship became much more beneficial for the employee.

How I Want to Be Coached Tool

So, how do you determine how an employee actually wants to be coached? You ask her! I have created a tool that allows you to ask the right questions. This tool will help your employee clarify and share her needs and expectations while in a coaching relationship with you, her direct reports, or her peers. The more your employee's needs and expectations are fully communicated, the greater the chance for a productive, developmental experience.

The key questions you should have your employees answer include:

1. The one thing I need most from my coach is:

   _____

2. Many things motivate me; however, my top three motivators are: _____

3. When you are coaching me, you can realistically expect me to: _____

4. I need and expect my coach to: _____

5. Your support for me can best be shown by: _____

6. Some developmental opportunities that you could assist me with are: _____

7. Additional information not covered above that would be important while coaching me is:_____

8. Considering my past managers or coaches, I'd like you to:

   • Stop:_____

   • Start: _____

   • Continue: _____

As you seek to understand how your employees want to be coached, make sure you listen to the answers to these questions, take notes, and apply this knowledge to your coaching and leadership style with each individual employee. Much like the Situational Leadership model, coaching should always be tailored to the individual's needs and wants.

So, how do *your* team members like to be coached?

» Do you really know how each of your direct reports likes to be coached?

» Do you know what motivates them?

» Have you peeled back the layers to truly understand the answers to the two questions above?

» Have you asked them?

» Have you written down how each of your direct reports likes to be coached?

» Do you review their answers before your coaching sessions?

The next question a Leader Coach asks himself is how *he* likes to be coached. For this to be effective, the Leader Coach should review the same questions from the How I Want to Be Coached Tool, first with himself and then with his boss.

Knowing the answers to the questions in the tool will help the Leader Coach's boss become a better coach to him. It will make both leaders more effective, enable the growth and development of the employee, and therefore ensure that the right style and type of coaching will be implemented. For more information on the tool or to get a copy, please go to **turbivillegroup.com.**

Coaching in the Moment: How to Observe and Assess a Leader Coach

One of the challenges most leaders face is that they have very few opportunities to see their direct reports actually coaching employees. Occasionally leaders will see their direct reports interact with their employees in meetings or during sessions that their direct reports lead. These are usually meetings where the direct report is providing instruction, feedback, advice, or sometimes counseling. Usually no true coaching occurs in these settings.

Most leaders are open to listening to stories of how a direct report coached an employee. Depending on how well the direct report explains how she coached, and how accurately she relates the actual coaching conversation, the leader will develop an internal story as to the effectiveness of the coaching. Since most leaders have not observed a live coaching session led by their direct reports, however, leaders tend to rely on their perception to determine which direct reports are effective coaches.

To solve this dilemma, one of the things that I implemented early in my career was an opportunity to watch my direct reports do live coaching with their employees. This practice was developed by one of my direct reports, Jon Snow. We called it "Coaching in the Moment," because it truly was time set aside to see a direct report coach an employee in a live setting.

This is the way it worked: I would join a meeting with my direct report and one of her employees. During this coaching session, my direct report would be conducting a business meeting discussing a few specific opportunities that her employee was focusing on. These could vary widely from customer opportunities, developmental opportunities for the employee, strengths that the employee had demonstrated, challenges the employee was having with her direct reports or peers, or discussing commitments and action items from a previous meeting.

The setup for the Coaching in the Moment is critical. I always sat next to the person being coached. This way she did not feel like two of us were staring at or interrogating her. I started the meeting by explaining that my purpose for being there was twofold. First, I was interested in the employee's development, and I wanted to get to know her better. This created a sense of trust that I was not there to catch her doing something "wrong" but that I was truly interested in her.

Second, I let the employee know that I was also there to observe the effectiveness of her boss's coaching. I set up this comment by reiterating how important coaching was to the organization—and to me. I let the employee know that everyone in the organization was coached by his or her direct supervisor and that we all needed to be open to being coached.

To lighten the mood, I always joked that the pressure was on her boss to demonstrate effective coaching! This made the employee being coached more comfortable. I also let the employee know that occasionally I would be jotting down notes about my direct reports' actual coaching. I assured the employee that I was *not* documenting anything about her.

Next, I let my direct report reiterate how important being a strong coach was to him. He would set the tone that this would be a natural, three-way conversation. It was vital that I participated in the conversation instead of just sitting there as a quiet observer. Throughout the discussion, I would ask follow-up questions of them both and show genuine interest.

At times during the coaching conversation, I would ask the employee if she was open to my thoughts. I would then share my thoughts on the issue and reinforce how important she was to the organization. I wanted to let her know that I cared about her success.

Resistance and Key Learnings

While there was considerable initial resistance among some employees to doing Coaching in the Moment, I stayed steadfast in my goal and vision to improving coaching effectiveness through empirical observation. My direct reports eventually all agreed to try it.

I set a goal for them to conduct one Coaching in the Moment per month. What happened was amazing! As they became more comfortable, they began to do several of these per month with their direct reports and employees. They recognized the value of seeing their direct reports coach in a real situation. It changed their perception of the importance of developing a strong coaching competency. It also demonstrated to leaders and individual contributors at all levels that coaching effectiveness was a priority. Over a short time, the leaders' coaching effectiveness and confidence significantly improved.

We learned many lessons from conducting Coaching in the Moments. For example, we recognized some misperceptions that we had of who were effective coaches. In one case, I thought my direct report was a great coach. He communicated his coaching to me consistently and impressively. Although I had not seen him coach, I was convinced that he was the strongest coach on my team.

But when I saw him coach live in a Coaching in the Moment, I saw something different. I saw a coach that was telling his employees what to do instead of asking effective questions that led to the employee's developing ideas and solutions. He was not effective at meeting the employee where she was in her development or coaching her based on her needs. He did not use situational coaching. This experience gave me the opportunity to provide coaching and feedback to my direct report to help him improve his coaching effectiveness.

A Leader Coach Coaches to Aligned Competencies

A number of books have been written about the importance of strengths-based leadership and how to focus leadership efforts on building strengths. While I mostly agree with the core thoughts around these principles in many such books on the market, one important element is clearly missing: what to do if your own strengths are *not* aligned with the needs of your organization.

We can categorize strengths in three parts:

1. What you do best—your personal branded strength

2. What you do better than other people—your competitive advantage

3. Your strengths are aligned with the organization's needs—the key to moving up in an organization

We all have something that we do really well. These strengths have helped us be successful. To use these strengths effectively and to advance further in our career, we first need to identify them. The next step is to develop a plan on how we can use these strengths to perform our jobs at a high level. As we develop and use our strengths, we will see both job and career growth.

What you do better than other people is a strength that can lead to a competitive advantage. I consider this the basis of your personal brand. When you have a competitive advantage, you can leverage it to be more effective and successful than most people. This is important because organizations will notice and value you. If your strength is unique, you can be sure that your organization will take note! In fact, a unique strength that is valued by your organization assures you that you will be needed and have a bright future in it.

If you are working for an organization, your strengths should be aligned with the organization's core competencies. If they are not, your growth and career will be stunted. For example, if you desire to move into a leadership position and one of the core competencies is inspiring and mobilizing a team, you work on developing this competency. Inspiring and mobilizing a team is critical for all leadership positions. The problem is that many individual contributors have never developed the ability to inspire or mobilize others. So, while they perform well as an individual contributor, they fail as a leader without this strength.

Early in my career, I led one employee who desired to rise to management rank. He was actually an outstanding individual contributor, but lacked some key leadership skills such as knowing how to coach and develop others and how to inspire a team.

Still, I took a chance on him, hoping I could help him develop the skills. Unfortunately, he wanted to be a super sales-representative and not a leader of other people. He wanted his team to do everything the way he did it. After all, he was extremely successful.

As you could have predicted, he did not work out as a leader. He could not build trust because he did not give his team autonomy. Fortunately, with the help of my coaching, he eventually recognized that he was a better individual contributor.

Over the years I have coached executives who fall into this same category. They excelled as individual contributors but after years of floundering as a leader of people still have not learned to inspire, mobilize, and coach employees effectively. They have skated by, by virtue of their technical skills alone. This type of leader creates a drag in the organization and her team. She should be coached up, placed in a role that fits her skills, or coached out of the organization.

If you are to be successful, you strive to identify your strengths and your competitive advantage. You ensure that your strengths are aligned with the organization's needs. When you do these things, you are poised for business success!

A Great Leader Coach Sets and Communicates Clear Expectations

A great Leader Coach sets and consistently communicates clear expectations. Describe what meeting expectations looks like—and what exceeding them requires. The clearer your expectations, the better chance your employees have to achieve them.

The Leader Coach is clear herself about the expectations. As an executive coach, I have found that many leaders struggle with setting clear expectations because they are not sure what their boss or organization expects from them.

I was recently coaching an executive from a Fortune 500 company. His boss had asked me to coach him on how to set clear expectations with his own people. As I progressed through the coaching engagement, it became obvious that he did not understand his boss's expectations of him or his team. Without this understanding, how could that executive set meaningful expectations? Unfortunately, I have found this common in organizations.

In this case, I coached my client to ask his boss what he expected of him. As he discussed expectations with his boss, it became clear to him—and he was able to set crystal-clear expectations for his team.

A Leader Coach understands, communicates, clarifies, and reinforces expectations. This can be done in the following ways:

1. Spend 1:1 time with direct reports to discuss expectations and their progress toward accomplishing the expectations.

2. Coach the direct report, which increases her chances of achieving the expectations. This includes asking effective questions like "What are my expectations of you and your team?" and "What do you understand about the expectations that I have for you?" and "How can I help you achieve them?" Finally, the Leader Coach asks: "What are your expectations of your team?" and "Tell me about the progress of your team."

3. The Leader Coach provides positive *and* negative feedback to the employee. This feedback is always genuine and candid. When goals and expectations are being met or exceeded, the Leader Coach should show appreciation to the employee. Certainly, there will be an opportunity to learn from the employee's success so that the Leader Coach can share learnings with other employees.

A Leader Coach who is super-clear on expectations, and also is a great communicator and reinforcer of expectations, stands a far greater chance of developing a high-performing team.

A Leader Coach Holds People Accountable

If you care about and respect your people, you will hold them accountable. The goal of coaching is to help employees improve performance by developing competencies and skills. A Leader Coach and the employee she is coaching demonstrate vulnerability when they are engaged in the coaching. It shows that they are both imperfect and open to improvement.

A Leader Coach is a role model of accountability. When she commits to do something, it is completed. If the Leader Coach needs help, she demonstrates humility by asking for it.

Great leaders recognize that increasing productivity and improving performance are an ongoing, consistent focus. The role of the Leader Coach is basically to meet and exceed expectations. The responsibility to maximize performance rests with the leader.

In one organization, I had a leader who was consistently a low performer. When I took over as her supervisor, I sat down with her to discuss her team's performance. She consistently blamed her previous manager for not supporting her and blamed her team for not meeting her expectations.

I let her know that I would give her a fresh start, but her performance had to improve. Despite ongoing coaching and feedback, she never changed her approach to the business or her team. Within six months, I had to terminate her.

When I let her go, she was outwardly angry and hostile. I neutralized the situation and I was patient with her. I let her express her feelings before she stormed out. While it is never easy to terminate an employee, there are times when it just has to be done.

The most interesting part of this story occurred a few years later. I ran into this former employee, and she pulled me aside to talk. I had no idea what to expect. What followed was a big surprise.

She thanked me for terminating her and said it was a defining moment in her life. It made her realize that she needed to make some changes. She shared with me how she was currently a top-performing leader in her new organization and realized how much she had learned from the situation with me. According to her, it was life-changing.

I learned a number of lessons from that experience. As a leader, we are doing employees a favor by holding them accountable even when the end result happens to be termination. I believe that most employees want to perform and do well. When they are chronic low performers, they are not happy. As leaders it is our responsibility to coach, inspire, and assist our direct reports to achieve high performance. When that fails, we need to step up and take action.

Sometimes, of course, leaders have to make tough personnel decisions. They need to appropriately coach up employees when they seem to have the will and the skill to do the job. At other times, leaders have to coach an employee out of the organization, especially if the employee lacks the will and desire to do the job. I will speak more about this later in the book.

Conclusion

As we have seen, the Leader Coach can increase productivity and performance through effective coaching. She coaches to competencies that are aligned with organizational needs. She asks questions that cause each employee to ponder and develop better solutions.

The Leader Coach takes the time to understand how each employee wants to be coached. She uses the Coaching in the Moment process to observe real-time coaching. She is humble, candid, and approachable, and she truly listens to employees. And she is comfortable with being herself.

The Leader Coach sets and communicates clear expectations that are aligned with the organization. She allows each employee the autonomy to complete tasks. She cares enough about her people to hold them accountable to her expectations.

Great Leader Coaches understand that the act of coaching and developing team members benefits them as much as the employees they are coaching. Remember: coaching involves mutual responsibility! Coaching involves two people who have the desire to grow and develop. If both parties are not engaged and motivated to improve, coaching will always fail.

Ask yourself these questions about being a Leader Coach:

- » Which characteristics of a Leader Coach do I possess?

- » How humble am I as a leader?

» What keeps me from being more authentic with my people?

» How can I mentor, especially new employees, in the organization?

» Do I know how each of my direct reports wants to be coached?

» Does my supervisor know how I myself want to be coached?

» How can I effectively use the How I Want to Be Coached Tool?

» How can I implement Coaching in the Moment with my leaders?

» How can I ensure that I am coaching to competencies that are aligned with the organization's needs?

6

Performance-Driven Leadership

> *"If you care about your people, you will hold them accountable for performance!"*

I Want to Win!

When I was a second-line leader, I would often ask new managers what their goal was for performance. Almost inevitably they would respond, "I want to win" or "I want to exceed expectations." My response was, "What do you want to win?" or "What are the expectations?"

This is what many leaders say when asked about performance goals. They are not sure what to focus on or how to create expectations for their direct reports that concentrate on professional growth and results.

Certainly, leaders are clear about goals and understand the steps necessary to achieve them. Goals are future-based. They are clear and specific, but more importantly the steps necessary to achieve the goals are crystal clear.

Great leaders recognize that achieving results is a process that is focused on what you can do in the present. Leaders and employees should ask the question, "What do I need to do today to achieve my goal?"

Performance-Driven Cultures

"Performance more often comes down to a cultural challenge, rather than simply a technical one."

–**Lara Hogan**, *Senior Engineering Manager of Performance, Etsy*

Leaders define, communicate, and model the behavioral changes that will create a performance-driven culture. There is a shared vocabulary throughout the organization so that employees understand the desired behaviors.

Cultural change is treated as a major business initiative. As leaders model performance-driven behaviors, employees will believe such change is important. When leaders recognize and reward performance-driven behaviors, employees will change their behavior to align with the culture. Leaders help employees achieve small behavioral changes. These wins will create momentum that, in turn, will lead to major change.

Organizational change starts with individual change. The challenge is that each individual's willingness and ability to change is different. Leaders shape the culture one employee at a time.

While leaders model and communicate the behavior, they do so in a people-focused way because, ultimately, it is employees themselves who will drive a performance-driven culture.

As noted previously, Costco is a great example of a high-performing culture. Its leaders are grown organically through leadership training received from executives and senior leaders. High expectations are set by the leaders, and goals are made clear.

The high level of the company's retention (94 percent) and engagement, much higher than that of its major competitors, has led to many consecutive years of significant growth. Additionally, a typical Costco employee generates about three times the revenue of a Walmart or Target employee

So, one wonders, why don't most organizations have a performance-driven leadership culture? It's because their leaders do not follow a structured coaching and performance process. They have not spent the time developing leaders so that they themselves can develop and sustain a high-performing culture.

Three Keys to Drive Performance

"Leadership is all about results."

–**Peter Drucker**

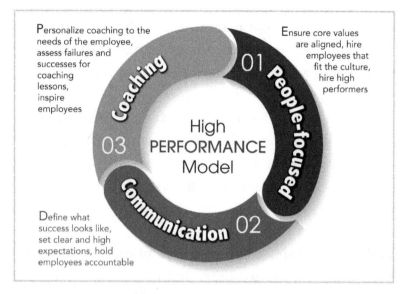

Figure 3: High Performance Model, by Eric Turbiville

As shown in figure 3, great leaders do three things to drive performance and win. These are activities and expected behaviors focused on the present that will lead to exceeding goals and expectations.

First, they are people-focused. They recognize that their employees are the core of the business. The results they are seeking can only be achieved through the people.

Leaders concentrate on decisions and commitments that are aligned with the organization's core values. Employees understand, believe in, and live the company core values and support the purpose of the company. When employees are aligned with the core values, are passionate about the products or services, and come to work every day energized and motivated, they will be far more productive and will drive performance.

Leaders build a team with proven high performers. They hire and then promote employees who have a history of high performance and collaboration. Teams that cooperate and share ideas and successes, work well together. They inspire each other to perform at a high level. They create an environment of team-wide trust and confidence.

It is imperative that leaders hire for cultural fit, which includes promoting and hiring employees who have consistently performed in previous roles. Andy Ajello, former senior vice president of Diabetes and Obesity Sales at Novo Nordisk, implemented a hiring rule that leaders could *only* hire external employees who had performed in the top 20 percent of their organization. This rule allowed the company to hire the best available talent in the industry.

According to a McKinsey article, "A recent study of more than 600,000 researchers, entertainers, politicians, and athletes found that high performers are 400 percent more productive than average ones. Studies of businesses not only show similar results but also reveal that the gap rises with a job's complexity. In highly complex occupations—the information- and interaction-intensive work of managers, software developers, and the like—high performers are an astounding 800 percent more productive." (Source: "McKinsey Global Survey: War for Talent 2000," refreshed in 2012; Scott Keller and Mary Meaney, *Attracting and Retaining the Right Talent,* McKinsey, November 2017, https://www.mckinsey. com/business-functions/organization/our-insights/attracting-and-retaining-the-right-talent)

Second, leaders communicate clearly and consistently. They define what performance and winning look like. They identify the actions that should be taken. They identify the skills and behaviors required to execute those actions. They ask, "What can I do now to execute my plan?"

They set and consistently communicate high, clear expectations. They have thought about not only what it will take to exceed goals, but also what should be done daily to achieve the result. They communicate these expectations to their subordinates consistently and frequently, especially during weekly coaching conversations.

They consistently hold their people accountable for high performance. They reinforce the behaviors and actions that are expected of employees. They recognize that success is not permanent and that the status quo is not acceptable. What got the leader, employee, or organization to where they are, will not get them to the next level of performance.

When it comes to agreed actions, leaders ask the questions, "When will you do it?" and "How will I know that you did it?" They expect their employees to return and report. This is a principle that puts the responsibility on the employee to follow up with the leader to report on actions they have committed to complete. When employees do not return and report, leaders follow up to ensure that the expected actions are executed.

Third, leaders are strong coaches. They personalize coaching. They understand how each team member wants to be coached. They recognize and reward activities and behaviors that lead to the desired outcome. They provide feedback and counseling when those behaviors and actions are absent.

A performance management system is in place to ensure that employees can and do perform the necessary actions and behaviors. Leaders support their employees by asking questions such as "What are you doing well and why is it working?" or "What can you do better and how will you do it?"

Leaders focus on inspiring and mobilizing their teams to action. They help develop the competencies of the team members while recognizing that the employee owns her personal development. They use every touch point with every individual on their team to inspire and mobilize them to exceed expectations.

Leaders regularly assess successes and failures. The study and evaluation of successes leads to more success. Many times, leaders expend energy and hours evaluating failures but never learn from successes. Failures are learning opportunities, too! It is critical that leaders understand what could have been done better, more often, or not at all. When leaders learn to assess successes and failures, they can set clearer expectations and coach more effectively.

The Importance of Hiring Great Talent

I coached one executive who shared with me news of a "great hire" he had made. This was someone he knew from a previous organization where they had both worked. He knew this employee was motivated and successful, but he was not sure how he would do in a slightly different leadership role.

When we discussed why he thought this leader was a great hire, he outlined how clearly the leader communicated with his team about expectations, set goals, and frequently reinforced them with his team. He provided feedback on their performance and "feed-forward" on how each employee could get to the next level of performance. He coached effectively and inspired his team. He held them accountable for performance. He hired people who were motivated to succeed and who fit the culture. He did all the things we have talked about that lead to high performance.

This employee did not merely excel at his first position. He later excelled in two other completely different executive leadership roles. And he continues to be successful as a leader because he follows the principles that lead to high performance.

Grit Wins Over Skill

"The first requisite for success is the ability to apply your physical and mental energies to one problem incessantly without growing weary."

–Thomas Edison

Work is full of challenges and setbacks. While we focus our time on developing skills and behaviors that lead to success, grit is a key factor for top performers in any position. Sometimes you just have to suck it up and get the job done.

Why do some people succeed while others fail? Talent alone does not guarantee success. Angela Duckworth has found that grit—a combination of passion and perseverance for a singularly important goal—is the hallmark of high achievers in every domain. She's also found scientific evidence that grit can grow. In her book *Grit: The Power of Passion and Perseverance*, she discusses this key quality and how it affects our ability to accomplish our goals and aspirations.

Duckworth writes: "Grit is the tenacious pursuit of a dominant superordinate goal despite setbacks." It is passion and effort exerted over a period of years. It is about pursuing a goal even when there have been disappointments and failures along the way.

So, what is "grit"? It's about showing up. It's about having passion for your goal along with an unwavering sense of direction and determination. It's about doggedly refusing to give up after a failure or setback. It's not about talent. It's about effort and the time we spend on achieving the goal that we are passionate about.

Anders Ericsson developed the term "deliberate practice," meaning the amount of time and energy we spend in the pursuit of expertise. He concluded that 10,000 hours seems to be the magic number of hours needed of deliberate practice to develop true expertise. To gain 10,000 hours, you need to display grit and determination. You will focus on doing what you need to do in order to master your skills and achieve your goals. Throughout all challenges, you have intrinsic motivation to persist in your pursuit.

I coached another executive who ran two businesses at the same time. She was determined to make both organizations succeed. She was raised in the Midwest and had a strong work ethic. Despite many challenges and obstacles, both companies were eventually highly successful. She was smart but, more importantly, she had the grit and determination to be successful.

Overall Motivation

Today, it is more critical than ever to keep your customer-facing employees engaged. After all, they are the ones driving the customers' experience. Yet most organizations are struggling to understand how to do this.

Lindsay McGregor and Neel Doshi wrote about the principle of total motivation as a way to improve revenue, cost, risk, and customer satisfaction.

"Why people work determines how well they work—that someone's motive for doing a task determines their performance. Our work has shown that if a person's motive is play (for example, excitement from novelty, curiosity, experimentation), purpose (the work matters), and potential (they are improved by the work), then their total motivation and performance increase. But if their motive is emotional pressure (shame, guilt, insecurity), economic pressure (mercenary behavior), or inertia (no motive), then total motivation and performance worsen." (Lindsay McGregor and Neel Doshi, "How Company Culture Shapes Employee Motivation," *Harvard Business Review,* November 25, 2015, https://hbr.org/2015/11/how-company-culture-shapes-employee-motivation)

McGregor and Doshi's research demonstrates that in order to have a performance-driven company, you need to focus on your people. Creating a great customer experience ultimately comes down to having great people and treating them right. You have a strong company purpose and a clear "Why" behind the company vision. You rely on understanding and appealing to what motivates your people.

Tool: What Motivates You?

Most leaders assume that money is the primary motivator for employees. The truth is that while making enough money to meet their wants and needs is important, it is not their primary motivator. In fact, most surveys find that developmental opportunities, autonomy, making an impact, and having a higher purpose are the key motivators.

If you are to be successful as a leader, you will need to understand how to inspire and mobilize your team. The only way you can do this effectively is to understand what motivates each of your people. And the best way to find out what motivates each employee is to ask and then listen! Here are some questions that you can pose to your employees to understand what motivates them:

1. Which part of your current job do you enjoy most?

2. Which part of your current job frustrates you the most?

3. Which part of your current job gives you the greatest sense of purpose?

4. When are your contributions to the organization's overall goals most inspiring to you?

5. You define your purpose for work as follows: In other words, you go to work because you want to:

   _____

6. How often does your leader recognize and reward you for your job performance?

7. What type of reward do you find the most motivating?

8. What does reaching your full potential look like? How can I help you achieve it?

9. What have past leaders done to inspire you?

Remember, you cannot really motivate anyone. All you can do is inspire your people, based on your understanding of their individual motivators. Leaders don't motivate, they inspire! If you would like more information or a copy of the "What Motivates You" tool, please go to **turbivillegroup.com**.

When I was a young sales leader, I first learned these lessons about individuals' motivators. On one occasion, I was trying to understand the motivators for one of my employees. Once we got past the first layer, which usually consists of money and supporting a family, I began searching for her real motivators. What I found was eye-opening.

She shared with me her desire to be one of the top performers in the organization. She knew she could do it and wanted to show her family and peers how great she was as an employee. As I discussed the likely obstacles to achieve this, she said that one of the obstacles was that she had a fear of standing in front of the entire company to be recognized for her performance. This was a problem because the top performers all had to stand up in front of the company to be recognized!

We spent time talking about how to overcome this obstacle. We made good progress, and I am happy to say that about one year later she stood in front of the entire company and her spouse to be recognized as one of the highest performers in the company.

I tell that story because it is our job as leaders to truly get to the heart of what motivates our people. Until we understand their motivators, we cannot effectively inspire them to perform at their highest level.

Measure Success

If it can be measured, it can be improved.

> *"Experience and intuition are still very important, but you have got to triangulate them with data. As I always say: 'In God we trust; everybody else, bring data.'"*
>
> **–Sim Tshabalala**, *CEO of Standard Bank*

The old adage "inspect what you expect" is as valid today as ever. Likewise, with the immense aggregate of data collected by most organizations, it is easier to measure execution across key performance indicators.

Almost all employees can improve any behavior, skill, or competency that can be measured. Leaders are responsible to ensure that these things get measured. They will make sure that financial, performance, and other objectives get measured, as well.

When leaders have data to measure success, they can compare it to behaviors and actions to find the gaps that need improvement. Likewise, leaders can see where employees have performed well and can then share those learnings with their teams and the overall organization. If you care about your people, you will use appropriate data to evaluate their performance.

Performance Management: Accountability

I supervised a new second-line leader who, early in his leadership role, had placed a low-performing employee on a performance improvement plan. During a meeting with the employee, he received pushback from him.

The employee only wanted to talk about the productive year he had five years previously. My direct report was a little taken aback by the response and was unsure how to respond. I happened to be sitting in on the meeting, so I helped him.

I responded, "We appreciate your performance five years ago and your contributions to the company since then. The reality is that your performance has not been acceptable the past year. Let's focus on how you can improve, moving forward."

This set the tone for a productive meeting that focused on the recent past and the future. I would like to say the end result was positive, but this employee decided not to change behaviors or to focus on improving, despite support and coaching from his supervisor. He left the team to pursue opportunities outside the organization.

Performance management is a leadership process. It all starts at the top. Top leaders believe in performance management. This requires them to spend time discussing performance with their direct reports. Top leaders coach direct reports and spend time developing them.

I coached one executive who never shared or discussed sales performance with his direct reports. In fact, I believe he had no idea how they were performing against goals and key performance indicators. He felt that his direct reports themselves knew how they were performing, so there was no reason to discuss performance until the year-end reviews. But he ran a sales organization!

Think about all his missed opportunities to recognize high performance, coach, and course-correct low performers. Needless to say, his organization was not a high-performance culture.

Great leaders model the performance-driven culture by providing direct reports the support needed to achieve organizational goals. Leaders communicate clearly and regularly about the organizational goals and how achieving or missing them will affect the organization.

Senior leaders expect the same behaviors from their direct reports and hold them accountable for modeling these behaviors and expectations to the rest of the company. All leaders will follow the lead of their direct supervisor, and these expectations will cascade throughout the organization by direct communication and, most importantly, by example.

A Few Steps to Create a Performance-Driven Culture

When the following things happen, you will create a performance-driven culture:

» Goals must be communicated clearly and frequently, and employees need to be told how they fit into the goals of the organization.

» Clear management of underperformance is needed to ensure that underperformers are managed either up or out of the organization.

» Open and regular discussions are held between employees and managers on performance. These discussions will not just occur during midyear and year-end reviews. Leaders also ask employees, "What is going well?" and "What needs improvement?" and "What do you need from your manager to achieve your goals?"

» Leaders at every level are held accountable for fostering a climate conducive to a performance-driven culture.

» Leaders coach employees effectively and consistently. According to the International Coaching Federation,

140

organizations with strong coaching cultures are twice as likely to be high-performing organizations.

> » Let people "fail forward and fail fast." Failures are looked at as learning opportunities rather than being incidents held against the employee. Let your employees take calculated chances. Reward innovation, and recognize risk-taking even when the end result is not ideal.

> » Leaders recognize and reward employees who live and model a performance-driven culture. Remember that intrinsic rewards are more important than extrinsic ones. Money is *not* the top motivator for most people. Recognition is one of the top motivators.

Leaders across all departments own the process of creating and maintaining a performance-driven culture. It is, in fact, the senior leaders who model the behaviors and expectations of the organization. A performance-driven culture starts at the top and is a product of the shadow of a leader, each leader creating a leadership shadow that reflects and models the desired performance.

Leaders hold their people accountable for performance. It is not enough to have strong competencies, although they lead to high performance. Ultimately, leadership is results-based. A leader who does not hold her people accountable is shirking her duties.

Improving Performance at TTUHSC

At Texas Tech University Health Sciences Center, leadership, led by Chief People Officer Steve Sosland, blew up the annual performance review process in favor of a quarterly coaching plan. The organization changed the compensation system by delinking pay increases to an annual review. Instead, they created opportunities for additional pay raises given to high performers.

Why? As Sosland visited several TTUHSC locations and asked how much time employees were spending on the annual review process, it ranged from 15 minutes for experienced employees up to 15 hours for newer employees who took the process more seriously. Meanwhile, managers were spending weeks to months preparing for the annual reviews. When employees were asked about the annual review process, they responded that they complied with it because Human Resources "made us do it."

Sosland and his team found that annual reviews were *not* indicative of true performance. In fact, what he learned was that managers generally gave better evaluations, because employees' pay was tied to the reviews. This resulted in inflated reviews that could not differentiate a high performer from a low performer.

The change that resulted was simple, yet significant. The annual review process was replaced with a quarterly coaching plan for all employees. Sosland remarked, "Everyone will have a plan to improve performance through a coaching plan." By implementing such a plan for all employees, the supervisor became a partner with each employee, and coaching became the tool to help improve performance. Coaching placed accountability squarely on the shoulders of each employee.

Conclusion

Leaders at every level hold employees and also themselves accountable for performance. Accountability means the leader will hold herself accountable and will allow others to hold *her* accountable. A no-excuses attitude permeates the organization. There is a people-focused and coaching-centered approach to performance.

Similar to a people-focused and coaching-centered leadership culture, a performance-driven leadership culture provides a significant competitive advantage.

Ask yourself these questions about being a performance-driven leader:

> » Have I clearly defined what winning means for my team?

> » How many of the three keys of high performance am I following?

> » What can I do to ensure that I hire high-performing people who fit the culture?

> » What motivates each of my employees?

> » What motivates me, and does my supervisor know about it?

> » How effective is performance management in my organization?

> » What steps have I taken to create and build a high-performing team or organization?

7

Hiring, Building, and Developing a Well-Coached, High-Performing Team

"Train people well enough so they can leave.

Treat them well enough so they don't want to."

–Richard Branson

Building a High-Performing Team

Individual performance is important, but only overall team performance drives an organization to reach its goals. Individuals work together to create a team that exceeds expectations.

High-performing leaders start by promoting and hiring employees who have consistently performed at high levels in every position they have held. One of the greatest predictors of success is high performance in previous roles. If an employee has been an average performer in previous roles, they will be average in her new role. Average performers may perform satisfactorily for a while, but eventually they will regress to the mean; in other words, they will eventually be average again.

The foundation of high-performing teams is trust in the leader. Employees trust the leader because they know she has their best interest at heart and wants everyone to be successful. The leader is competent, acts transparently, and possesses integrity.

Leaders understand and define what high-performance behaviors look like. They model, communicate, and reinforce these behaviors with employees. When high-performance behaviors are demonstrated, leaders recognize and reward the behaviors to reinforce them. Success should be celebrated. When employees fail to execute high-performance behaviors, leaders coach and provide feedback.

Leaders set and consistently communicate clear, high expectations. Employees are clear about what is expected of them. They understand what success looks like. Leaders communicate all the information necessary for employees to perform their jobs successfully. Additionally, goals should stretch employees to perform at their best.

High-performing teams feel united in purpose. Every team member is focused on high performance. There is camaraderie and an esprit de corps. Each employee has the same goal of doing her best within a team framework of excellence.

When employees fear the unknown or feel paralysis about taking action that leads to performance, ask them, "What is the worst thing that can happen?" Often when people think of the worst-case scenario, they can see that it is not as bad as they thought. Once they articulate their fear, they can address it head on.

Employees who cannot meet individual expectations are coached up or coached out of the organization. Leaders demonstrate that they can make tough decisions. If underperformers are not removed from an organization, high-performing employees lose respect for the leader.

Leaders provide employees the Why and What of their roles and empower the employees to determine How they accomplish goals. This autonomy inspires the employees to perform at a peak level.

Employees and leaders provide each other the resources and guidance they need to succeed. There is cohesiveness and support throughout the teams within the organization.

Leaders understand their role in organizational performance. Every leader in an organization performs in ways that help the organization achieve its goals.

Building a High-Performing Team Is a Decision

"The single biggest constraint on the success of my organization is the ability to get and to hang on to enough of the right people."

–**Jim Collins**

Leaders make a conscious decision either to create a high-performing team or to accept mediocrity. It is an active, thoughtful decision. Too many leaders, through their failure to make decisions and take affirmative actions, choose mediocrity.

Make the decision *now* that you will build a high-performing team. If you have not been doing the things necessary to build one, you will find resistance from some of your employees. These are, however, usually the lower performers. You should be focused, persistent, and strong enough to overcome the resistance and to do the things that will fortify your team.

At the heart of the decision to become a high-performing leader is the desire to be your best. You desire that each member of your team be her best, too. This requires hard, smart work.

So, what do you do if your team is only average? First, you recognize it and develop a plan to take action. Are there members of the team who need to be coached up? Members who need to be coached out?

These are tough questions, but the most difficult question the leader should ask herself is "Am I an average or below-average leader?" If the answer is either, then the leader has self-work that needs to be done. She needs to develop her leadership and coaching skills as she coaches and helps her employees on this journey.

As I have mentioned earlier, there is a principle called regression to the mean. Even average or below-average employees perform well at times. The reality is that eventually they will return to the level of their previous performance. Conversely, consistent high performers may have a short span of poor performance, but unless something fundamentally has changed, you can expect their performance to improve again.

I remember as a new executive I once inherited a below-average team. Some of the leaders were strong but the others were below average. My desire, of course, was to have a high-performing team. I had built and developed such teams before. So, I made a conscious decision that I would not accept mediocrity and that I would build a strong team. Then I rigorously followed the principles to develop one. If this is your desire and decision, this chapter will show you how to do it.

So, what is the most important step in developing a high-performing team?

Hire for Cultural Fit

"Shaping your culture is more than half done when you hire your team."

–**Jessica Herrin**, *Founder, Stella & Dot*

"Hire character. Train skill."

–**Peter Schutz, former CEO of Porsche**

Hire for fit first, then for competencies. You can teach skills and competencies, but you cannot teach cultural fit. For example, if you have a coaching culture, hire leaders who know how to coach effectively. If you want high performance, hire people who have consistently performed at high levels.

Leaders understand the DNA of top performers and hire like-minded, skilled employees who fit the organization's culture.

The most important thing a leader does is to make the right hiring decisions. Appropriate new hires will fit the culture, have emotional intelligence, be honest, have integrity, and show eagerness to learn and develop.

When I hire team members, I look for people who have different strengths than me. I want someone who will complement my skills and challenge me to think differently. Why? I already have me. I don't need another me. My experience is that diverse teams provide smarter solutions and perform better than less-diverse teams.

"Seventeen years ago, the case for emphasizing raw talent was expressed by a team from McKinsey and Company in their classic report 'The War for Talent.' Their conclusion was this: 'in the new economy, competition is global, capital is abundant, ideas are developed quickly and cheaply, and people are willing to change jobs often. In that kind of environment all that matters is talent.... Superior talent will be tomorrow's prime source of competitive advantage.'

"In that study, some of the top factors listed by managers as being necessary for winning the war for talent were things such as:

» Give high potentials the bulk of development opportunities

» Put high potentials into jobs prior to them being ready

» Eliminate the least effective performers

"However, from our perspective this advice does not tell the whole story. We believe organizations can generally function well by hiring good, solid people as long as they ensure the organization has effective leaders throughout." (Jack Zenger, "By the Numbers: Superior Leadership Produces Higher Return Than Superior Talent," *Forbes,* October 31, 2014, https://www.forbes.com/sites/jackzenger/2014/10/31/by-the-numbers-superior-leadership-produces-higher-return-than-superior-talent/#cfd538d2fe5e)

Think of all the challenges that a CEO faces. Guess what their number one concern is?

"'Failure to attract and retain top talent' was the number-one issue in the Conference Board's 2016 survey of global CEOs—before economic growth and competitive intensity." (Scott Keller and Mary Meaney, *Attracting and Retaining the Right Talent,* McKinsey, Organization, November 2017, https://www.mckinsey.com/business-functions/organization/our-insights/attracting-and-retaining-the-right-talent)

Another McKinsey article states, "A whopping 82 percent of companies don't believe they recruit highly talented people. For companies that do, only 7 percent think they can keep them." (McKinsey Global Survey: "War for Talent 2000"; extensive research conducted 1997–2000; survey of more than 12,000 executives at 125 midsize and large companies)

The article goes on to say that "More alarmingly, only 23 percent of managers and senior executives active on talent-related topics believe their current acquisition and retention strategies work." (*The State of Human Capital 2012: False Summit*, a joint report from McKinsey and the Conference Board, October 2012, McKinsey.com)

Herb Kelleher, cofounder of Southwest Airlines, once said, "We will hire someone with less experience, less education, and less expertise, than someone who has more of those things and has a rotten attitude. Because we can train people. We can teach people how to lead. We can teach people how to provide customer service. But we can't change their DNA."

Too many times in my career I have heard leaders justify keeping someone who is a high performer but struggles to embrace and live the values of the company. Some leaders seem to overvalue high performance and to simply justify poor behavior. This is not acceptable leadership. Employees with poor behaviors and attitudes are removed.

If you have someone who doesn't live the values of the company, act quickly. If you do not, you risk losing the culture on your team and organization. Companies make a serious mistake when they hire or promote leaders who do not fit the culture, even when they are high performers. Doing so leads to company-wide cultural change and an erosion of company values.

It is just as critical to resist keeping a chronic low performer so there will be a "warm body" in a specific role. I have heard leaders say, "I would rather have a person in a role than to have an opening." This is how a low-performing culture is established. Your high performers do not *want* low performers on their team. You should not either!

It behooves leaders to only hire A-players who fit the culture. You are wasting your time as a leader if you hire mediocre people and expect them to perform at a high level.

Onboarding for Performance

Once, when I was brought in as a new executive hired from outside the organization, I was immediately assigned both a mentor and an onboarding expert. My relationship with the mentor resulted in a long-term business relationship that lasted my entire time with the organization. He taught me about the politics of the organization, how to succeed in it, and many insights that made me a much better executive.

I also had a separate trainer. The onboarding trainer focused on ensuring that I got off to a quick start and excelled in my new position. He was a former senior executive, so he knew what it took to succeed as an executive and recognized the importance of the first 12 to 18 months in the role. He reinforced my job responsibilities and showed me how to network within the organization. And he ensured that I formed relationships with key people.

The combination of a mentor and an onboarding trainer helped me move through the learning curve far more quickly and successfully. I immediately formed working relationships with the right people, including my peers.

Effective onboarding ensures that new or recently promoted employees get off to a quick start. Onboarding requires leaders to pay attention to the needs of the employee and the organization. High and clear expectations are established immediately. Employees need to understand what is expected of them in their new roles.

A mentor and a trainer are typically assigned to every new employee. This may be one person filling both roles, or multiple people. It is critical that the new employee feels a connection with his peers and her boss. When new employees feel a connection with other employees, engagement and retention increase. They will feel like they are part of the organization.

New or recently promoted employees have a clear understanding of their role. It is the leader's responsibility to make sure the mentor and the trainer understand the employee's role and that they reinforce it during the onboarding process.

Effective onboarding results in higher engagement and less turnover. Since the new employee feels connected to the team and boss, he will be less likely to leave the company.

Onboarding also ensures that the new employee will be a good cultural fit. Team members, mentors, and trainers will know quickly if the new employee does not meet cultural requirements. If he does not fit the culture, the supervisor should take immediate action.

The result of effective onboarding is a happy team, because all members have participated in the process. It is also critical that leaders listen to the feedback about the new employee. By listening to feedback from the trainer, mentor, and team members, leaders will know if they made a good hiring decision.

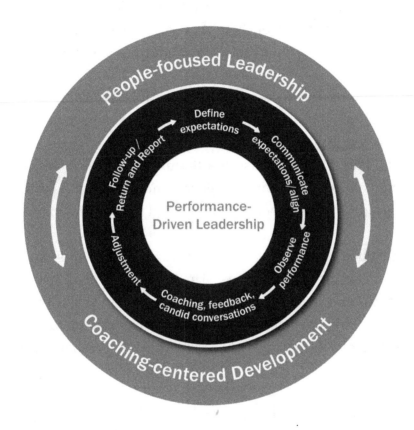

Figure 4: Performance-Driven Leadership Cycle, by Eric Turbiville

Define and Set Clear, High Expectations

Leaders have one opportunity to set high, clear performance expectations, so they must get it right the first time. It is easy to lower expectations later, but virtually impossible to increase them.

155

Leaders cannot be ambiguous about their expectations. Unfortunately, many are just that. This attitude demotivates and confuses employees. According to Gallup surveys, about 50 percent of employees strongly agree that they know what their leaders expected of them. Leaders are able to answer the question "Are my employees clear about my expectations?"

I once coached an executive from a Fortune 500 company who, according to his boss, struggled with setting clear expectations for his team. His boss felt that he was less effective as a leader than he should be because his team was not sure what was expected of them. His direct reports, and my client as well, felt frustrated because expectations seemed to be a moving target.

As I coached this executive, I soon realized that his boss had never set clear expectations. He was unsure of his boss's expectations; therefore, he did not know how to set them for his team. This caused a cascade effect throughout his part of the organization, because there was no clarity about what to focus on.

So, we spent time discussing how to clarify expectations with his supervisor. The answer was simple: *Ask*. It sounds remedial, but when leaders are unclear about expectations, they ask questions to seek clarity.

At first, his boss felt annoyed that my client did not understand what he expected. As more conversations and communication occurred, clarity began to emerge. My client was ultimately able to fully understand what his supervisor wanted. This allowed him to clarify expectations with his team.

Too many times in my career I have seen leaders fail to establish high expectations. They think that expectations can be adjusted later. The truth is that leaders immediately establish an environment in which employees are challenged with high expectations. When expectations are high, the top performers will respect the leader. They appreciate that the leader sees both great and poor performance. Top performers also appreciate it when low performance is not tolerated.

Once the expectations have been set, leaders consistently communicate and reinforce them. It is not enough to state the expectations once. Leaders regularly communicate and measure employees against expectations. When employees meet or exceed the expectations, leaders recognize and reward them. This sends a signal to the organization that what is asked of them is being measured and suitably rewarded. If employees fall short of expectations, leaders provide coaching and feedback. If necessary, course corrections are done quickly.

When a leader defines and sets clear expectations, they gain alignment with their employees. This process involves employee understanding and buy-in to the expectations. When employees understand and buy-in, they are far more likely to achieve them even when the expectations stretch the employee to go beyond what she initially thought she could accomplish.

Observe Performance, Behaviors, Skills, and Competencies

It is the leader's responsibility to observe each employee, so as to gain understanding and insight into their performance, observable behaviors, skills, and competencies. There are many ways to observe an employee, especially when the leader and employee are based in the same office. This can be done every day as the leader observes the employee's daily actions.

When the employee is located remotely, it is more of a challenge to observe her. If the leader supervises other leaders, Coaching in the Moment is a great way to observe the leader's employees. There is more about Coaching in the Moment as an effective tool for second- and third-line leaders in chapter 5.

Leader Coaches use every touch point with employees to listen, learn, teach, coach, and inspire. The greatest impact a leader will have occurs during one-on-one interactions. Be prepared for every interaction, and have a plan for what you can do to affect and positively influence the other person. Leaders are vigilant about finding opportunities to assess and evaluate other leaders, so they know how to coach and provide feedback.

Conduct Candid Conversations through Coaching and Honest Feedback

As a Leader Coach evaluates an employee, it is critical that candid conversations occur in a timely manner. Verbal feedback or coaching should be provided immediately. Written coaching reports or emails should be completed promptly and sent to the employee.

At Novo Nordisk, Andy Ajello, a former senior vice president of Diabetes and Obesity Sales, changed the name of "Field Ride-Along Reports" to "Field Coaching Reports." This put an emphasis on the importance of actually coaching employees and not simply providing feedback or doing a recap of the time spent with the employee.

Additionally, Ajello set an expectation that written "Field Coaching Reports" would be sent to the employee by the leader within 48 hours. This reinforced the coaching with the employee so that it would be both memorable and actionable.

When providing written feedback or coaching to an employee, the report should be aligned and consistent with the verbal feedback that is provided. I have seen many written coaching reports that were inconsistent with the verbal coaching and feedback. At times, leaders can be more direct and bolder with the employee in writing than they were during the verbal discussion. When leaders do this, it not only creates incongruency in coaching and feedback, but also results in the employee's losing trust and confidence in the leader.

Will vs. Skill

Will is the desire to accomplish a task or job. When an employee does not have the will to do a job, the leader has a candid conversation with her. When will is absent and a job or task is not new to the employee, it is time for serious intervention, coaching, counseling, and potentially even the dismissal of the employee.

Skill, by contrast, is the possession of the capabilities and competencies required to accomplish a task or job. It is important to recognize that most people can be taught and learn skills when they have the will.

159

I once supervised a second-line director who struggled with inspiring his team and driving performance. Despite extensive coaching and support, this director felt really frustrated and took his frustrations out on his team. Team morale and performance were, not surprisingly, abysmal.

In an effort to help with performance and to support him, I brought in a team of directors and home office personnel to help assess the business to see how we could help him grow it. After the team evaluation, the conclusion was that his team was missing opportunities to grow the business, relationships with key customers were poor, and the leader's strategy changed every month, causing his team to become confused.

As the team debriefed and shared their opinions with my direct report, he became visibly upset and dejected. He clearly did not want to hear their opinions.

After the meeting, he pulled me aside and shared his feelings with me. His words were telling. He said, "I do not have the desire to do this job anymore. I have tried everything I know how to do, and I can't do it." I tried to discuss his emotions and feelings of inadequacy, but he had made his decision. He had lost his will to do the job.

Now, this is a clear case of low will plus low skill. This director should never have been promoted into his position. He was not ready. No amount of training or coaching can make up for a lack of desire. He was not the right person for the job. I removed him from the position within a few weeks.

Course Corrections and Adjustments

As a plane's pilot makes hundreds of course adjustments throughout a flight, leaders need to be agile and flexible enough to allow employees to make their own course corrections. These will happen naturally as the employee aligns with the leader's expectations, changes her behaviors, builds her skills, and develops her competencies.

I recall an employee who reported to me. He possessed excellent analytical skills, but his coaching and leadership skills were average. So he worked hard at improving his leadership skills, based on the coaching I provided. Specifically, I worked with him on how to become a more proactive coach.

After one of our Coaching in the Moment sessions with a first-line manager, I noticed him adjusting his coaching and being more proactive. He was not just letting the manager ramble on; rather, my leader was actively listening and proactively managing the conversation. At one point in the session, my direct report realized he had missed an opportunity to provide better coaching and feedback to his employee, so he course-corrected and circled back in the discussion to provide the appropriate coaching and feedback.

Leadership and coaching are iterative processes that require constant course corrections and adjustments. There *are* no perfect leaders or coaches. Rather, each of us is given an opportunity daily to improve and to become more-effective leaders.

Follow-Up—Return and Report

When an employee commits to take action, whether it be changing a behavior, improving a skill, or completing a task that will bring her closer to achieving a goal, it is her responsibility to return and report to her leader. Follow-up is vital and necessary for an employee to be held accountable for action and change.

If the employee fails to follow up, the leader is accountable for ensuring that the employee took the action she committed to take. This failure by the employee should result in a candid conversation with her to reinforce the expectation that in future she will return and report on a consistent basis. The leader should highlight the importance of her knowing how the employee is progressing against completing actions.

At the heart of the performance-driven process is a constant, consistent reinforcement and alignment of the leader's expectations of each employee. As you saw in figure 4, the process of communicating with and helping her team become high-performing employees is a continuous cycle. It starts with defining and setting clear, high expectations; providing candid feedback and coaching; making specific changes that result in high performance; and placing the responsibility on each employee to follow up with the actions she committed to take.

Develop your People

"Leaders don't create followers, they create more leaders."
–Tom Peters

The CFO asks the CEO "What if we coach and train our people and they leave?"

The CEO responds, "What if we don't and they stay!"

–Anonymous

For many years in the business world, the argument has been that people leave their boss, not the job. As a result, leaders have long been criticized when high performers leave their team. The truth is that people leave jobs, leaders, companies, and even cultures.

One of the top reasons for leaving jobs is the perceived lack of developmental and growth opportunities. Therefore, leaders and companies have developmental plans, career maps, and growth strategies in place to keep employees challenged and motivated. Leaders are accountable for the development of their employees. They create growth and development opportunities for employees.

Your responsibility as a leader is to develop future leaders, not followers. Leaders do this by investing time developing employees, not merely for their current role but also for future roles. This is accomplished through effective coaching and mentoring.

Some organizations prefer to promote from outside the organization, especially when their talent pipeline is substandard. Other companies such as Costco and EBQ, a company focused on outsourced sales and marketing for B2B SaaS and tech organizations based in Austin, Texas, have chosen to *only* promote leaders from within the organization. They have set up internal systems and processes to make this happen.

For example, Costco developed Costco University, where senior leaders coach, teach, and train future leaders. New leaders emerge from the ongoing training and coaching prepared to lead a store or even to go on to greater responsibility in the organization.

EBQ is also committed to and has invested heavily in developing employees. It relies on internal training and coaching, but, more importantly, most of its development focuses on experiential training. Future leaders are given opportunities to develop on the job as they face real business situations, challenges, and opportunities.

EBQ offers weekly training classes, taught by directors and vice presidents, that can be attended by any employee. This training follows the approach of a "chute" (employees looking for new roles and responsibilities) and a "ladder" (employees seeking promotion within their own team). One component of this training includes mentoring from managers and directors.

These classes are offered during lunch hour or before or after work. By attending, employees show their commitment to get promoted, key leaders have the opportunity to assess and grow their employees' competencies, and the whole process reinforces a culture that values internal promotions.

Leaders inspire employees. They appeal to the motivators of each individual employee. They consistently bring out the best in each employee. Leaders are focused on developing trust by being open and transparent. Transparency, in turn, opens employees to being inspired by leaders. And that helps employees become agile learners.

If a key employee does leave, leaders need to ask some deep questions. One question they should ask is, "Did I provide developmental opportunities for the employee?" Another question that should be asked is, "Did the employee thrive in the culture—both the company culture and the immediate team culture set by me?" One final question that can add valuable insight is "Did I recognize the employee when he did something well?"

Focus on the Process

Some leaders believe that if you focus on winning, it will happen. No! You define what winning looks like, you coach to the skills and behaviors required to accomplish it, and you always hold people accountable.

Leaders should not even *try* to focus on winning or being number one. Instead, they should focus their team on the *process* of being successful. During my career I have seen leaders—including myself!–tell their team that the goal is to finish at the top and to exceed expectations. The problem is that some people do not know how to do this. They simply may not have the behaviors and skills to achieve their goal.

165

The role of us leaders is to set clear expectations and then coach to the behaviors that lead to success. It is our responsibility as leaders to teach our people what must be done, which skills need to be developed, and which behaviors need to change.

Should we focus on goals? Yes, with the understanding that the problem with that approach is that goals are sometimes actually in the control of other people. If you worry about things you cannot control, they will adversely affect what you *can* control.

So, what *can* you control? Behaviors and skills are both in your control. You develop and cultivate the behaviors and skills that will make you successful. You should ask yourself, "What can I do today to change my behaviors and develop the skills I need to succeed?" Or "What can I do today to accelerate my personal performance and to do my best?" If you take this approach, you will get closer to what you want to achieve.

Do your best by developing the skills and behaviors required for success. But be patient with yourself, because some behaviors take time to develop. As the late, great basketball coach John Wooden said, "Giving our all, doing our best, is all we can do."

In reality, succeeding is more important than winning. We focus on the specific behaviors, skills, and actions required to become the best version of ourselves to exceed expectations. Success occurs in the process, not just in winning the race. Success is a journey.

As the Spanish novelist Miguel Cervantes wrote, "The journey is better than the end." It is a process that begins with understanding ourselves and identifying the behaviors we need to change to be successful.

Conclusion

Building a high-performing team or organization is a decision that each leader must make. A process is followed to create and sustain the team. At the heart of all high-performing teams are leaders and employees who are fully committed to excellence.

When leaders hire employees who both fit the culture and have demonstrated a history of high performance, they set a foundation for a strong team. Expectations are clear and constantly reinforced. Employees follow up with their leader to report their progress.

Leaders are focused on coaching and developing the competencies as well as performance of employees. Leaders understand the process that leads to high performance, so they consistently coach and teach this process to employees.

Ask yourself these questions about building a high-performing team:

> » What does making the decision to build a high-performing team look like to me?

> » How do I ensure that I hire high-performers who are cultural fits?

167

» Who on my current team fits the description of being a high performer and is also a cultural fit?

» What am I doing about those who do not fit the description?

» Who on my team lacks the will to do her job?

» How can I teach my employees their responsibility to return and report on commitments they have made to me?

» What am I doing to develop my team members so that they can improve their performance?

8

The Leader's Role in Employee Engagement and Retention

"If you are lucky enough to be someone's employer, then you have a moral obligation to make sure people do look forward to coming to work in the morning."

–**John Mackey**, *CEO, Whole Foods Market*

Engagement is an outcome of your corporate culture. It is the result of how an employee feels and operates within the culture. It is how comfortable, motivated, and passionate employees are about your purpose, and how they work based on the culture.

High employee engagement occurs when employees are personally inspired and motivated by your culture. It is what happens in the hearts and minds of each employee on a daily basis that determines engagement

Most employees want to do their best, but is your culture designed to help this happen? Are your leaders engaged enough to care about their employees' engagement? If you have low employee engagement, look in the mirror. Ask yourself, "What can I do to increase engagement?" Remember, engagement occurs one employee at a time. This is an individual exercise, not a group project.

What Gallup Says about Engagement in the Corporate Workplace

For almost 20 years, Gallup polls have showed that about 70 percent of employees are *not* engaged. Think about that! If your company is typical, every day, most of your employees come to work and are really not concerned about doing their best. Most of them are not happy about your culture or growth opportunities and are definitely not concerned about the corporate bottom line.

But there is good news! Employment engagement is on the rise in the United States. According to the 2018 Gallup report, the level of engaged employees has increased by 6 percent over the last decade. This equates to approximately 8 million more workers who are engaged, energized, and connected to their organizations.

The report states that 34 percent of the workforce are engaged. Only 13 percent of the workforce is actively disengaged, the lowest in several years. The remaining 53 percent of the workforce are not engaged.

Why Does a High-Engagement Culture Matter?

According to Gallup, "Organizations and teams with higher employee engagement and lower active disengagement perform at higher levels. For example, organizations that

170

are the best in engaging their employees achieve earnings-per-share growth that is more than four times that of their competitors."

Gallup goes on to report, "Compared with business units in the bottom quartile, those in the top quartile of engagement realize substantially better customer engagement, higher productivity, better retention, fewer accidents, and 21% higher profitability." (Jim Harter, "Employee Engagement on the Rise in the U.S.," gallup.com)

Additionally, "In a Towers Watson study of 50 companies over a one-year period, organizations with high employee engagement had a 19 percent increase in operating income and nearly 28 percent growth in earnings per share (EPS). Conversely companies with low levels of engagement saw operating income drop more than 32 percent and EPS decline 11 percent." (Eric Mosley, "How Employee Engagement Drives Business Success," Chief Executive, March 2011, http://chiefexecutive.net/how-employee-engagement-drives-business-success/)

Other statistics stand out: "Related surveys report that 73 percent of employees are 'thinking about another job' and that 43 percent were more likely to consider a new one than they had been a year earlier." (*Appirio*, "This year in employee engagement 2016: Trends to watch," blog entry by Jiordan Castle, March 7, 2016, appirio.com)

Qualities of a High Employee-Engagement Culture

I was once an executive in an organization where employees were highly engaged. This was the case because senior leadership truly cared about its people and lived the purpose and values of the company. Senior leaders tried to get to know employees at all levels in the organization. It did not matter if you were an assistant, a clerk, or an executive. Everyone was treated with the same respect.

The senior vice president of sales personally knew many sales representatives and first-line managers. He remembered their names and details about their lives. They felt so comfortable with him that they would call or text him about challenges and opportunities. He knew what was going on in the sales force. He cared about his people. He was people-focused. He lived the values and culture of the organization.

In high-engagement cultures, leaders become vested in the success of the employees. They support employees and help them feel safe. In turn, employees trust their bosses. Leaders help employees grow and develop. Leaders take the time to coach their employees.

As a result, employees feel happy and satisfied with their jobs. This means the company performs better. They look forward to going to work each day. Leaders listen to employees' feedback and their ideas. Employees feel like they have a voice in decisions that are being made. Employees are motivated, feel engaged, and do great work because leaders support their growth and development.

Employees are passionate and inspired by the purpose of the company. They are advocates of the company. They tell everyone they know how great the company is. They are magnets that attract new employees who fit the culture. They are great corporate ambassadors.

Impact of a Low Employee-Engagement Culture

I worked in an organization where senior leaders were indifferent to most employees, especially anyone who was more than one level below them. Engagement in this organization was extremely low, and employees struggled with respecting the leaders because of the way they were treated.

I remember my boss in this company explaining to me the importance of forming a relationship with a specific senior executive in order to get promoted. So, I set out to meet and get to know this executive.

I found the perfect opportunity. I arrived early to a reception and the only person there was this senior executive. I was excited because I knew how hard it was to get quality time with him.

As I approached him, he looked up and saw me. His facial expression and body language seemed to scream, "Please do not come talk to me!" When I shook his hand, he did not make eye contact. I engaged him in conversation, but he was indifferent.

Eventually someone he knew walked in the room. He looked up, saw this person, and immediately walked away from me while I was in midsentence. It was so bizarre that I started laughing.

Now, I believe I am emotionally intelligent and can read situations well. Maybe it was bad timing or perhaps he just did not care. I believe it was the latter. I was two levels below him, so I could not help him. This is the type of uninspiring and disrespectful leadership behavior that leads to low engagement.

The reality is that low employee engagement is a result of a culture that fails to inspire employees. In such a culture, leaders do not live the organizational vision or, worse, the vision simply does not appeal to employees.

Low employee engagement leads to poor performance. When employees lack passion for their job, company, products, or services, they are less likely to put forth their best effort. If employees do not buy into the company's vision and purpose, they will have a low motivation to perform. Likewise, they will not hold themselves accountable for their work, nor will they have high expectations of it.

Low engagement leads to less innovation as well as to resistance to change. Since we are all in an evolving business marketplace, innovation is critical, and change is guaranteed!

Low engagement leads to poor collaboration, resulting in compromised work, subpar communication, and ineffective relationships. In addition, employees with low engagement usually bring negative attitudes to the workplace and typically also have poor relationships with peers and supervisors. This negativity is a culture killer!

Watch Out for Employee Entitlement

If there is one potential negative thing that can occur in a people-focused organization, it is employee entitlement. This occurs when some employees begin to feel that a company owes them because they are being treated well or the organization itself is performing well.

I have seen this happen in some organizations. Attentive leaders nip this attitude in the bud. Just because an organization cares about you, it does not owe you everything.

Employees who feel entitled lack emotional intelligence and maturity. They are too immature or inexperienced to recognize a great culture.

EBQ has been recognized by Inc. 5000 as a Hall of Fame member. Since 2012, *Inc.* has recognized it for five of the previous seven years as one of the fastest growing small companies in the United States. Additionally, since 2011, the Austin *American-Statesman* has recognized EBQ as one of its Top Work Places in five of the previous seven years.

At EBQ, Tim Edwards, the CEO, implemented a four-day workweek. It was designed so that employees could have more personal time. By working additional hours Monday through Thursday, employees were given Friday off.

At first, it was reported that employees felt excitement and increased engagement. While front-line employees had freedom on Friday, leaders were still working that day to preserve and grow business. What started out as an intentional benefit for employees soon began to hurt customers and the business. Although the early stages of the initiative resulted in higher employee productivity and engagement, eventually customers did not get the attention they needed, and revenue decreased.

When the organization decided to reinstate a five-day workweek, some employees felt upset. Even though meetings were conducted to explain the decision, there were employees who just felt entitled to the four-day workweek they had got used to. A few even chose to leave the organization, a very shortsighted decision given that few organizations have a four-day workweek.

As Edwards explained, "The four-day workweek caused us to lose customers and growth. The lost growth reduced employees' promotional opportunities." In an organization where internal promotions based on meritocracy prevail, the four-day workweek hurt employees as much as customers and the organization.

Why People Leave Their Jobs

"We want to turn inventory, but not our people.... People are happy with a job for more reasons than money. There's generally a pride in the organization."

–**Jim Sinegal**, *Founder and former CEO, Costco*

In 2018, over 42 million people left their jobs. Two of the most cited reasons were the lack of recognition and the lack of growth and developmental opportunities.

Research performed by the O. C. Tanner Institute found that:

» 79 percent of employees who quit their jobs claim that a lack of appreciation was a major reason for leaving.

» 65 percent of Americans claimed that they weren't recognized even one time last year.

» 82 percent of employees feel their supervisor doesn't recognize them for what they do.

» 60 percent say they are more motivated by recognition than money.

(David Novak, cofounder and retired chairman of Yum! Brands and cofounder and CEO of oGoLead, https://www.nbcnews.com/better/lifestyle/here-s-no-1-reason-why-employees-quit-their-jobs-ncna1020031)

As your employees recognize that you appreciate their efforts, they will be motivated to do more. When you commend and recognize employees, be specific. Tell them what you appreciate, what they did, and why you appreciate it.

In other exit surveys, former employees list four additional reasons for leaving that leaders should consider.

First is a toxic work culture. If employees feel that they are compromising their values as a result of working with the company, you have serious problems. Remember that, when people leave because of a poor company culture, they can become your strongest adversaries. Unhappy former employees can tarnish your brand. Certainly, your reputation will be hurt through their negative social media postings and reviews.

Poor leaders and management are what people think of when they say an employee leaves because of their manager. Most surveys no longer directly link this to the number one reason that employees leave a company.

The question that human resource leaders should be asking is, "Are employees staying because leaders are becoming better?" The answer is clear. Since two of the major reasons employees leave companies is the lack of growth and development opportunities and the lack of recognition, clearly leaders are still failing. Both of the top two reasons for employees' leaving are reflections on leadership. When there is no growth or recognition, employees feel disconnected from leadership.

The second primary reason for leaving one's job is that it didn't match with the job listing or the job description and details that were told to the employee during the interview process. When this happens, the employee usually leaves fairly quickly. While there is always some ambiguity in every job, the basic job requirements should be clear at the start.

The third reason is the lack of clear expectations around the role, which causes employee frustration. There is no excuse for any leader to fail to set and communicate clear expectations.

This is a key part of seeking employee engagement and performance. How can employees accomplish a goal if they do not know what the goal is?

The fourth reason given leaving one's job is that there is no onboarding process or mentoring program for new employees. When a new employee does not have strong onboarding, leaders miss an opportunity to help them be successful. Strong onboarding leads to a shortened learning curve, a fast start on the job, and future enhanced performance.

As author Bruce Tulgan remarked, "If you want your superstars to stay working for you, you have to ask, 'What can I do as a leader and manager to keep you on this team?' Don't wait until they are thinking about leaving!"

It is vitally important to engage and retain key talent. Leaders understand why employees stay with the organization, and what may cause them to exit the organization. Again, the Stay Interview I discussed in chapter 2 can help answer these questions. If a course correction is necessary, leaders act quickly.

Employee Happiness = Greater Profit

Eric Siu wrote, "Although you don't have to be a math whiz to understand the correlation between happiness and productivity, the Department of Economics at the University of Warwick [U.K.] found that happy workers are 12 percent more productive than the average worker, and unhappy workers are 10 percent less productive. In fact, unhappy employees cost

American business over $300 billion each year. So, it literally pays to make sure your employees are happy."

Siu continues, "Statistics from New Century Financial Corporation indicate that employees who are actively engaged in their job, i.e. happy, produce better results. For instance, account executives at a banking company who were actively disengaged produced 28 percent less revenue than those who were engaged. On the other hand, companies with happy employees outperform the competition by 20 percent, earn 1.2 to 1.7 percent more than their peer firms, and are 2.1 percent above industry benchmarks. Happy workers are also more likely to solve difficult problems faster." (Eric Siu, "It Really Pays to Have a Rich Company Culture," *Entrepreneur,* October 1, 2014, https://www.entrepreneur.com/article/238640#)

Göran Ando, M.D., former board chair at Novo Nordisk, adds, "Happy, motivated employees stay with the company and grow and develop. These are the best people to have interact with your customers."

Employee Unhappiness = Less Profit

Eric Siu went on to ask, "Are you starting to see the picture? Unhappy employees are disengaged at work, which leads to negative attitudes and low productivity, and ultimately affects your business' bottom line.

"In fact, low-level engagement within companies results in a 33 percent decrease in operating income and an 11 percent decrease in earnings growth, whereas companies with high-level engagement have a 19 percent increase in operating income and a 28 percent increase in earnings growth." (Eric Siu, "It Really Pays to Have a Rich Company Culture," *Entrepreneur*, October 1, 2014, https://www.entrepreneur.com/article/238640#)

Engagement Is a Personal Choice

Engaged employees stay with their company longer and are more productive, resulting in a significantly greater impact on the corporate bottom line.

Engagement is a choice made by each employee. She has to decide if she is passionate about the company's purpose and vision. Leaders can try to inspire and motivate employees but, in the end, actual engagement is a personal decision.

During my career, fortunately I only worked in one low-engagement culture. While I had a subculture that promoted engagement, it was a struggle for me to keep my direct reports engaged with the company. Frankly, I knew—and my direct reports could tell—that I personally had trouble staying engaged with the company.

So, I decided to just coach my employees to do their best to stay engaged. I believed then, and believe now, that no matter what is going on around you, you should do your best to be fully committed and perform at your highest level. Don't damage your career, resume, or reputation by performing at a substandard level merely because of a poor company culture. If you need to, seek opportunities outside the organization.

Effective leaders are engaged enough to care about employee engagement. If they are not motivated to care about that, their employees will fall into the class of disengaged employees, meaning they will not be sufficiently productive to contribute significantly to the corporate bottom line. These are the leaders that you need to help exit the organization with all deliberate speed.

Six Talent Magnets

In its 2018 Global Culture Report, the O. C. Tanner Institute lists Six Talent Magnets. When these magnets are present, employees will be engaged. They are as follows:

1. *Purpose*—knowing that their work is connected to something bigger that adds value and makes the world a better place. This is about understanding and being congruent with the corporate purpose and the Why behind the company.

2. *Opportunity*—having a voice in decisions even when they may not have a vote. It is about doing challenging, meaningful work,

3. *Success*—the feeling of playing on a winning team and experiencing the thrill of personal and team victories again and again. Even small victories make a difference. Leaders find ways to help employees feel the excitement of winning.

4. *Appreciation*— knowing that their effort, results, and contributions are noticed, valued, and recognized by peers and leaders. Remember, the lack of appreciation

is one of the major reasons people leave jobs. Leaders show and communicate gratitude and appreciation for employees' efforts and accomplishments.

5. *Well-being*—feeling cared for at work beyond just physical fitness; feeling emotionally healthy and socially connected. The reality is that emotionally satisfied and happy employees are more productive.

6. *Leadership*—feeling that their leader is an advocate, coach, and mentor. Feeling inspired, supported, and encouraged by those in charge. Engagement is about having strong leaders who inspire and appeal to the motivators of each individual. (Adapted from the O. C. Tanner Institute, 2018 Global Culture Report, https://www.octanner.com/insights/articles/2019/8/14/everything_you_need_.html)

EBQ: Example of a High-Engagement Culture

The Texas-based company EBQ uses multiple touch points to engage employees. Senior leadership conducts company meetings, referred to as "firesides," to communicate with and engage employees. The majority of the time during the firesides is dedicated to responding to employee questions. These are questions that the leadership team has not formally prepared for, so the result is usually a fluid and candid conversation.

Tim Edwards, EBQ's longtime CEO, believes that "The firesides keep employees connected to the company vision. They also allow employees to hear from the source about company goals, purpose, and why specific leadership decisions have been made. Employees hear directly from leaders, so they don't

THE PERFECT LEADERSHIP TRIAD

have to guess why things are happening." The firesides allow employees' input and help them feel that they have a voice in the company, even if they may not have an actual vote.

Having clear, candid conversations with leaders is a vital practice for promoting employee engagement. The more that employees understand about decision-making and the purpose of the organization, the more engaged they will be. The more they hear from leaders, the less likely they will need to fill in the information gaps by using fictitious or blatantly wrong information from "water cooler conversations."

EBQ made a decision early in the organization's existence that it would invest in people and create opportunities for growth. According to Edwards, "EBQ has a meritocracy based on what you can do and are willing to do when it comes to promotions."

The company's weekly training classes, open to all employees, are a great example of providing them with many developmental opportunities. Additionally, effective leadership coaching is individualized, based on the needs of the employee. Each employee completes the Myers-Briggs assessment so that managers can better understand the employee's personality and learning style.

The organization's approach is no-nonsense within a professional environment. While there are no Ping-Pong tables or product giveaways like those at many high-tech companies, the employees do have a fun environment where they can grow and develop. As Tim Edwards said, "You can only give away so many Yeti's. What employees really want is to sit down with their supervisors to discuss their career path."

EBQ's leadership candidness, opportunities for career growth, and internal promotions seem to be working well to keep the company's employees engaged. Most importantly, according to Edwards, "We are able to retain our A players."

Novo Nordisk: Engagement through Values and Purpose

Novo Nordisk has consistently been ranked as one of the Fortune 100 Best Places to Work, as well as one of the best places to employ working mothers. It has a long history of sustaining a culture that inspires and motivates employees to serve a higher purpose. Internal employee surveys highlight an engaging culture maintained by highly engaged employees.

According to the company, "The Novo Nordisk Way" is a foundation on which decisions are made that affect the business, its customers, and of course its employees. Novo Nordisk explains these beliefs on its website this way: "[The Novo Nordisk Way] describes who we are, how we work and what we want to achieve, and sets a clear direction for our company and our employees."

The organization conducts a "values audit" of each affiliate every one to six years, to ensure that the organization, in every part of the world, lives up to the values found in the Novo Nordisk Way. The process is referred to as Facilitation.

Facilitators "travel around the company to interview employees, managers and internal stakeholders, looking into documents and local business practices to assess to which degree the units are run in accordance with the Novo Nordisk Way. And just as they identify areas for improvement, these facilitators also highlight and share best practices throughout Novo Nordisk.

"Consolidated observations and trends are then reported to Executive Management on a half-yearly basis and the Board of Directors annually. It's an assurance that helps safeguard our strong company culture of responsible and sustainable business practices and ensures that the Novo Nordisk Way exists not only as words, but also as the way we run our business around the world." (Novonordisk.com)

These facilitations reinforce and help preserve a high-engagement culture. When the organization or an affiliate is not operating in an acceptable manner, facilitators can identify it and help with a course correction.

Conclusion

The presence of high employee engagement can create a more competitive organization and can also lead to a competitive advantage in the marketplace. Employees need to be inspired and motivated by your culture and purpose.

Engagement is a personal choice that is made by every employee, including the leaders. If the leader is not engaged, her employees will not be fully engaged.

High engagement results in higher productivity, better retention, and increased profitability. When employees are happy, customers are happier—and profits grow.

Ask yourself these questions about engagement and retention in your organization:

» What percentage of my employees are engaged?

» Which qualities of a high-engagement culture do I have in my team or organization?

» Why do people leave their jobs in my organization?

» How happy are my employees?

» Why are they happy?

» What am I doing to engage and retain employees?

» How aligned are my employees' values with my values and those of the organization?

9

Culture and Brand: How They Impact The Perfect Leadership Triad

> *"Culture is the behavior that results when a group arrives at a set of—generally unspoken and unwritten—rules for working together."*
>
> **–Edgar Schein**

Anne Rhoades is a former Chief People Officer of Southwest Airlines and president of People Ink. Southwest is a model of a culture of excellence that follows the pattern of the above epigraph. According to her, leaders drive values, values drive behaviors, behaviors drive culture, and culture drives performance. (Anne Rhoades with Nancy Shepherdson, *Built on Values,* Jossey-Bass, 2011, p. 15)

Every organization has a culture. Culture is a collective personality of the members of a company or a team. It consists of a set of shared values and behaviors that determine how business is accomplished. It is all about how employees treat each other.

A company's culture has three components. First are the written and unwritten (usually unwritten) that are revealed in the words,

189

actions, and behaviors of the company's leaders. The second consists of the values of a company. It is critical that the values of the employees be aligned with the values of the company. If there is a disconnect, you have employees who will be disengaged and ineffective. The third component of a company culture establishes what is acceptable behavior within an organization. The behaviors of employees, especially leaders, set the tone for the culture. The actions and behaviors of senior leaders have the biggest impact on the culture. They shape the behavior of the people.

Why Your Culture Is Important

> *"My job was to be a keeper of the culture."*
>
> –**Andy Ajello**, *former Senior Vice President, Novo Nordisk*

Every company has a culture based on its history, environment, and past and current leaders. Culture determines how decisions are made and how strategy is developed. Culture is the lifeblood of any organization. Every leader has the responsibility to be a keeper of her company's culture.

When I asked Göran Ando, M.D., former chairman of the board at Novo Nordisk, about his company's culture, he said, "The culture at Novo Nordisk is uniquely strong. It is the strongest culture I have seen in any company." Ando went on to say, "As I traveled the world meeting with Novo Nordisk employees, the culture was the same whether I was in China, Denmark, or the United States."

This cultural consistency across an organization is critical for a culture to survive and thrive. Novo Nordisk's culture has survived many years, especially under the leadership of both Ando and former CEO Lars Rebien Sørensen. This is because leaders at every level of the organization lived and breathed the culture.

Andy Ajello, former senior vice president of Diabetes and Obesity Sales at the company's operations in the United States, added, "The Novo Nordisk culture allowed you to stay true to who you are. It allowed you to be yourself." He went on to say, "As the sales leader in the United States, my job was to be the keeper of the culture."

If leaders are not living your culture, the employees won't, either. They are like children in one respect: they see right through their leaders! They hear what you are saying but they will not necessarily do what you are not doing.

It is important, therefore, that your people have a voice in their work even though they may not have an actual vote in how things are done. As long as they get the opportunity to provide input, they will most often buy in to what you are doing as a leader. When employees believe their voice is heard, they will trust you.

Leadership as a Conduit of Culture

"Employees make hundreds of decisions on their own every day, and culture is our guide. Culture tells us what to do when the CEO isn't in the room, which is of course most of the time."

–**Francis Frei and Anne Morriss**, coauthors of Uncommon Service: How to Win by Putting Customers at the Core of Your Business

191

Remember that culture is always based on beliefs, values, and behavior. Leaders examine their own personal values. When they are clear about their personal values and have clarity into the organization's values, and when these values are aligned, the result is improved employee engagement.

Leaders obviously have the greatest influence on any organization. In fact, employees will usually mimic and follow their leader's words and their behaviors. So, the most effective way to change a culture is to change the way leaders lead and behave! It all starts with leadership.

Characteristics of a Strong Culture

Organizations don't build sustainable cultures. People do! This is why being people-focused is so important.

In a strong culture, leaders are highly engaged and passionate about the purpose of the organization. They recognize, of course, that their employees are the actual drivers of the business. In other words, the organization is people-focused.

Leaders are authentic. This may be the single most important characteristic of an effective leader. With authenticity come candor and honesty. When leaders possess both these qualities, employees are more likely to be open about their challenges and as a result will become more motivated and engaged.

Leaders are clear about expectations. Every employee understands her leader's responsibilities and goals. Coaching, feedback, and follow-up are consistent and expected of leaders. The organization invests in coaching and developing its employees.

Organizations with strong cultures have high levels of cooperation and collaboration. Employees work together to ensure organizational success.

Leaders and employees own their behaviors, actions, and performance. They recognize that their contributions affect the organization and help the company achieve its goals. Employees own their performance at every organizational level.

Strong cultures provide leaders and employees with autonomy, while at the same time requiring accountability. Empowering employees is an essential part of the culture. Accountability is both personal for each employee and shared as a team and an organization.

Failure in a task or project is viewed as a learning opportunity. You either succeed or you learn. Employees are not punished for making mistakes. Instead, effective leaders use the situation as a teaching and coaching moment.

Finally, a strong culture is performance-driven. The leaders and employees recognize that they have a job to do and that their work will make the organization more profitable. When a company has a culture that is performance-driven, it can afford to grow, can produce opportunities for employees to develop, and can meet the customers' needs.

Reinforcing Your Culture

> *"Culture is the environment in which your strategy and your brand thrives or dies a slow death."*

–**Shawn Parr**

Most organizations have a slogan. For example, Bristol-Myers Squibb's is "Our company's mission is to extend and enhance human life by providing the highest-quality biopharmaceutical products." The company is focused on developing and commercializing pharmaceutical products that help extend and save lives.

Southwest Airlines' most recent slogan is "Low fares. Nothing to hide. That's transparency." This focuses on the company's long-time strategy of competing on price. More important, it positions the company against other major airlines that have hidden costs such as flight change fees and baggage fees.

Many organizations have legends, either true or exaggerated. For example, Fred Smith, founder of FedEx, was known for making a desperate trip to Las Vegas to gamble so that he could make payroll, early in the company's history.

The Legend of IBM

> *"You win or you learn."*

–**Tim Edwards**, *CEO, EBQ*

The following legend about Thomas Watson Sr., founder of IBM, reinforces the belief that his company has traditionally forgiven thoughtful mistakes.

The predecessor of IBM managed to survive the Great Depression. Gambling on a likely post boom, Watson maintained IBM's employment levels by increasing inventories even when there was little demand for its services. As a result, excess machinery and parts crowded basements and filled every nook and cranny of Endicott's warehouses in New York, the original location of the company's manufacturing, research, and development.

Some on the company's board of directors, because of this, were lobbying to remove Watson as IBM's president. So, he desperately needed these inventories sold.

A very large government bid, approaching a million dollars, was on the table. The IBM Corporation—no, Thomas J. Watson Sr.!—needed every deal. Unfortunately, the salesman involved failed. And IBM lost the bid. That same day, the sales rep showed up at Watson's office, sat down, and rested an envelope with his resignation on the CEO's desk. Without looking, Watson knew what it was. He was expecting it.

He asked, "What happened?"

The sales rep outlined every step of the deal. He highlighted where mistakes had been made and what he could have done differently. Finally he said, "Thank you, Mr. Watson, for giving me a chance to explain. I know we needed this deal. I know what it meant to us." He rose to leave.

Watson met him at the door, looked him in the eye, and handed the envelope back to him, saying, "Why would I accept this when I have just invested one million dollars in your education?" (Taken from Peter E. Greulich, Volume III of *Tom Watson Sr. Essays on Leadership: We Forgive Thoughtful Mistakes*)

This anecdote illustrates that the most important reinforcement of culture comes through the behavior of leaders, especially top leaders. Their behavior will be closely observed by employees to see if it is congruent with the stated culture.

Enron's Debacle

The giant energy trading company Enron's motto was "Respect, Integrity, Communication and Excellence." Its vision and value statement included the following: "We treat others as we would like to be treated ourselves.... We do not tolerate abusive or disrespectful treatment. Ruthlessness, callousness, and arrogance don't belong here."

But in the 1990s and early 2000s, Enron would demonstrate what a corrupt, ethic-less culture breeds. The company's gigantic accounting fraud and pervasive corporate corruption came to be illustrative of a toxic, dishonest culture. Its ultracompetitive environment was in fact a breeding ground of greed and a demonstration of a corporate mentality of "do whatever is necessary to make money."

Employees will follow leaders who demonstrate trustworthiness and ethics in their behavior. The leaders at Enron did the opposite, and their employees mindlessly followed them. What resulted from these illegal behaviors were prison sentences for key executives and a loss of billions of dollars for investors. Ruthlessness, arrogance, and the lack of integrity abounded in the organization.

Starbuck's Crisis

Coffee megalith Starbuck's mission is "to inspire and nurture the human spirit—one person, one cup and one neighborhood at a time." Its core values include "Creating a culture of warmth and belonging, where everyone is welcome. Acting with courage, challenging the status quo and finding new ways to grow our company and each other. Being present, connecting with transparency, dignity and respect."

On April 12, 2018, two black men were arrested in a Philadelphia Starbucks coffee shop on suspicion of trespassing after a Starbuck's employee reported them; they had bought no coffee. While they were doing nothing wrong, they were still arrested. What happened next was an excellent example of how leadership reinforces a culture.

"Sensing the urgency of a racial profiling situation quickly spiraling out of control, Kevin R. Johnson, the chief executive of Starbucks, did what every good leader does when faced with a PR crisis. He sprang into action, on a Saturday."

He genuinely apologized, took responsibility, and called for immediate action to resolve the situation.

"These two gentlemen did not deserve what happened, and we are accountable. *I* am accountable," he said. With the public outcry of discrimination getting louder each day and others calling for the shop manager's job, Johnson acknowledged a potentially deeper and systemic management issue that placed the blame squarely on his shoulders.

Demonstrating the leadership strength of humility and redirecting the media's attention on him, Johnson stated: "Now there's been some calls for us to take action on the store manager. I believe that blame is misplaced. In fact, I think the focus of fixing is this: I own it. This is a management issue, and I am accountable to ensure we address the policy and the practice and the training that led to this outcome."

So, on May 29, at his direction, Starbucks closed more than 8,000 of its stores for several hours. During that time, nearly 175,000 of its employees participated in racial-bias training designed to prevent discrimination in their stores.

Think about what the Starbuck's employees—especially the other leaders—learned about their culture. It was authentic, and their CEO, Kevin Johnson, was willing to take the blame and responsibility for the situation. He acted with courage and conviction to ensure that everyone knew they were welcome at a Starbucks. (Taken from Marcel Schwantes, "Starbucks's CEO Showed a Classy Example of What a Great Leader Does When Managing a Crisis," *Inc. Magazine,* April 17, 2018, https://www.inc.com/marcel-schwantes/starbuckss-ceo-showed-a-classy-example-of-what-a-great-leader-does-when-managing-a-crisis.html)

During a major crisis like this one, employees will always watch to see if their leaders' reaction is aligned with the culture. In the Starbucks case, senior leaderships' actions were indeed aligned with the culture. The leaders' behavior demonstrated both authenticity and integrity.

In any business situation, if the behavior is not aligned to the culture, the culture will not stand on solid ground. A leader's misaligned behavior when a crisis occurs signals to all employees that the culture is not authentic.

As Milton Goggans, a former senior vice president of Bristol-Myers Squibb, said, "People need to feel comfortable that their leaders are consistent, especially during a crisis."

Changing an Ineffective Culture

So, what do you do if you determine that your culture is not effective and needs to be changed?

An organization needs to establish its vision, values, and purpose. These should be defined clearly so they can be easily understood by employees at all levels.

Great companies often use stories and metaphors to illustrate and clarify the new culture. The stories solidify the values of the culture. Leaders then have ongoing communication with employees about that culture.

When employees' actions are aligned with the new culture, they should be recognized and rewarded. New cultural stories will emerge as employees align with the new culture.

The behaviors of leaders necessarily should always align with the corporate culture. After all, they are the ones who set the example of expected behaviors. Leaders hire people who fit the new culture. If hiring mistakes are made, they are quickly corrected. Likewise, employees who continually resist and refuse to accept the culture change are quickly removed.

Culture change happens one person at a time. Whether to support a culture change is a decision that each employee makes over time. The leader's responsibility is to inspire and appeal to what motivates each employee, to get them onboard.

Reshaping a Culture: Texas Tech University Health Sciences Center

"Culture is a result of how employees treat each other."

–**Steve Sosland**, *Chief People Officer, TTUHSC*

The Texas Tech University Health Sciences Center had a culture of fear of retaliation. So, the organization decided it was time to shake up the culture and create one with a safe environment where employees were excited and not afraid to come to work. Steve Sosland, the organization's chief people officer, was brought in to help. As a professional culture disruptor, his job was to evaluate and lead a culture change.

His first step in early 2018 was to travel to all 28 locations of the organization to listen, observe, and ask about the TTUHSC culture and what employees would like it to consist of. After gathering information, he brought together a diverse group of no fewer than 104 employees to help set the foundation of a new, values-based culture.

Sosland placed these employees in small groups. He took them through a visualization exercise where each employee was asked to go back in their minds to their youth. They were asked to think of someone who was teaching them what they should or should not do. In other words, they would reflect on the values they were taught in their youth.

The groups then came together and, after lengthy discussion, identified 15 value-based words that these reflections had in common. These words were grouped based on similarity. Finally, the group voted on five words they wanted in their culture.

After defining these words, Sosland asked the question, "How will you know when you are living these values?" The answers were vital to understanding how to establish and maintain these values within the organization.

Sosland then conducted 91 town hall meetings over the next three months to share the values and create a grassroots, bottom-up campaign for the new values-based culture. The goal was not only to establish a new culture but also to integrate the five values into all processes throughout the organization.

To do this, his team established five groups called Value Integration Teams. These consisted of a recruiting, hiring, and retention team; a recognition team; a people development team; a communication team to help brand the culture; and a team to establish TTUHSC as an employer of choice.

The recognition team, led by the human resources department, created a Weekly Hero Huddle. This weekly meeting's purpose was to recognize employees who had demonstrated the values of the organization during the previous week. In other words, their purpose was to catch people doing something *right*.

At the first meeting, Sosland was the only one who brought an employee to the meeting to be recognized. It appeared that the employees' pervasive fear of retaliation lingered in the organization, so leaders were concerned about the new process.

Over time, however, leaders realized how impactful the meeting was for employees' being recognized. They eventually began accompanying employees to the meeting to recognize them more widely. Sosland and his team built excitement around the meeting, and news of it spread throughout the organization.

Here is one story that Sosland shared. "One of the employees recognized had only been with the organization for six months when he was brought into the meeting to be recognized for living the values. When he received the follow-up letter at his home signed by human resources specifically recognizing what he had done well, not only was he touched but so was his father.

"After receiving the letter, the employee related his story to the Weekly Hero Huddle. Six months previously he was on the street, addicted to drugs, and his girlfriend had just become pregnant. His father reluctantly let him move into his house. His life was in a downward spiral, but he committed to turn things around.

"He began to change his life and got the job with TTUHSC. When he received the letter, it became proof of his turnaround. In fact, when his father read the letter, he told this employee how proud he was of him. This was the first time his father had ever said these words to him."

What a wonderful example this is of how a culture can be changed for the better! What an even better example of how people can reshape and create a culture in which employees feel excited and proud to come to work.

Word spread fast about the new culture. In 2019, TTUHSC was voted, for the first time, one of the top 100 universities to work for. In fact, the number-one reason now given by new employees for joining the organization is its admirable culture.

Culture as a Competitive Advantage

"Corporate culture is the only sustainable competitive advantage that is completely within the control of the entrepreneur. Develop a strong corporate culture first and foremost."

–**David Cummings**, *Cofounder, Pardot*

Not only does your culture affect your brand, it can also give you a significant competitive advantage, because it is typically inimitable. No two leadership teams or founders are really alike, so a company's culture truly is the shadow of a leader. The leader casts a shadow of influence over the entire organization and sets the tone for how employees will act and interact with each other and customers.

Your culture can, however, be your principal disadvantage if you have built a poor culture or let a good one deteriorate. The good news, though, is that a culture can be corrected if senior leadership is committed to make the changes and take the necessary actions.

As I have said throughout this book, the best cultures are focused on people, coaching, and performance. The Perfect Leadership Triad brings all the components of an effective culture into one culture.

Your Brand

> *"It takes 20 years to build your reputation and five minutes to ruin it. If you think about that you'll do things differently."*
> **–Warren Buffet**

Your brand is your reputation! I am not referring to your tangible products or services. I am referring to what your organization is known for.

This is the question leaders should ask themselves: "When our employees are talking about working in our organization, what do they say?" This same question should be posed to employees to see what they think your company brand actually is.

If the leader wants to know her personal brand, a similar question can be asked of others: "When you think of me, what do you think of?" This is a great question to ask your peers, supervisor, and direct reports.

Every organization has an employee experience and a customer experience.

The employee experience begins with how employees are treated by the organization. It is part of your company brand. Remember, leadership is about being people-focused. It is about understanding that how you treat your employees is how they will treat your customers. If leaders are arrogant and inconsiderate, employees will act that way with customers. Likewise, if employees know you care about and respect them, they will be respectful to your customers.

The customer experience starts with your employees, especially the front-line ones. Creating a great customer experience begins with hiring great people and treating them well. Hire for attitude. You can train employees on skills, but you cannot train for attitude.

Once you hire the right fit for your organization—people who truly value the purpose of your organization—then your responsibility is to take care of your people. When employees are aligned with the purpose of the organization and are passionate about it, they will be more engaged and committed to your goals. It is vital that leaders be aligned with the organization's purpose. If they are not, employees will be far less likely to be engaged.

Organizations should always be clear about employee expectations and should allow employees to act as they think suitable. If you want employees to be problem solvers and customer advocates, give them the freedom to do it.

Leaders model and coach employees on the expected behaviors. If this does not occur, employees will not believe that the organization really values the behaviors. Leaders then recognize and reward employees who do exhibit the expected behaviors.

Communication and reinforcement of the brand are both consistent and frequent. This is accomplished through the behaviors and actions of leaders. Your brand is critical to promoting and marketing your organization, including to potential employment candidates, current employees, and customers alike. Leaders should always want the brand to demonstrate that their organization is the best place to work.

Southwest Airlines: Model of the Customer Experience

Consider an instance of how Southwest Airlines went above and beyond for a specific customer in 2011. A man had booked a last-minute flight to Denver to see his daughter the day after her three-year-old son had been murdered. Due to heavy traffic, he arrived at the airport gate 12 minutes after the plane was scheduled to leave, but the pilot had specifically waited for him before taking off.

In news report, the events went like this: "Last night, my husband and I got the tragic news that our three-year-old grandson in Denver had been murdered by our daughter's live-in boyfriend.

"He is being taken off life support tonight at 9 o'clock and his parents have opted for organ donation, which will take place immediately. Over 25 people will receive his gift tonight and many lives will be saved.

"This morning, after only a couple hours' sleep, my husband and I began to make all arrangements to get him to Denver to be with our daughter. He is currently on business in LA and is flying Southwest.

"While his employer, Northrop Grumman, made arrangements to get his ticket changed so he could get to Tucson today (which he had to do in order to not spend any extra money) I called Southwest to arrange his flight from Tucson to Denver so he would be stepping off one plane and getting on another.

He has several free flights with them so I couldn't really do it on the website. The ticketing agent was holding back tears throughout the call. I'm actually her step-mother and it's much more important for my husband to be there than for me to be there."

"In LAX [Los Angeles International Airport], the lines to both check a bag and get through security were exceptional. He got to the airport two hours early and was still late getting to his plane.

"Every step of the way, he's on the verge of tears and trying to get assistance from both TSA and Southwest employees to get to his plane on time.

"According to him, everyone he talked to couldn't have cared less. When he was done with security, he grabbed his computer bag, shoes and belt and ran to his terminal in his stocking feet.

"When he got there, the pilot of his plane and the ticketing agent both said, 'Are you Mark? We held the plane for you and we're so sorry about the loss of your grandson.'

"The pilot held the plane that was supposed to take off at 11:50 until 12:02 when my husband got there.

"As my husband walked down the jetway with the pilot, he said, 'I can't thank you enough for this.'

"The pilot responded with, 'They can't go anywhere without me and I wasn't going anywhere without you. Now relax. We'll get you there. And again, I'm so sorry.'

"My husband was able to take his first deep breath of the day.

"I don't know any other airline that would have done this." (Christopher Elliott, "Southwest Airlines Pilot Holds Plane for Murder Victim's Family," *Elliott Advocacy*, January 10, 2011,

https://www.elliott.org/blog/southwest-airlines-pilot-holds-
plane-for-murder-victims-family/)

This customer and his family were greatly touched. Can
you imagine the impact that pilot's decision had on other
Southwest employees and customers when they heard about
it? This is what customer experience is all about. This is what
establishing your company as the best place to work looks like.

The Power of Employee Advocates

Employee advocates act as ambassadors of your organization.
These are people who understand, live, and breathe the
organization's purpose. They are passionate and engaged.
They look for reasons to stay with the organization. These
advocates are your gateway to the outside world, especially to
customers and future employees.

Leaders should ask the following questions:

If your company offers retail products or services, do your
employees and their families and friends buy from you? This
indicates whether those employees are true advocates.

Are your employees there for a paycheck, or do they truly
believe in your purpose as a company? This is a barometer of
just how engaged the employees are and whether they commit
to your vision.

Do your employees represent you well with customers and
fellow employees? Or do they speak poorly of the company with

friends and on social media? If your employees are trashing you on social media, you have brand and cultural problems.

Benefits of a Strong Brand

"A brand for a company is like a reputation for a person. You earn reputation by trying to do hard things well."

–**Jeff Bezos**, *Founder and CEO, Amazon.com*

Many clear benefits accrue from a company's having a strong brand. Companies with attractive brands attract better talent to the organization. People want to work for it because the corporate reputation is stellar and because it aligns with the values of the potential employee.

A strong brand attracts and retains profitable customers. The main reason this happens is that the customers' interactions with employees are positive and uplifting. Happy employees attract happy customers. And happy customers spend more money on your products and services.

Employees will be more engaged in companies that have established a strong brand. I wrote about engagement in the previous chapter, and suffice it to say that when values, purpose, and beliefs are aligned among employees and companies, the employees will be engaged. Engagement results in more revenue and greater employee retention.

Team retention is also increased as a result. Employees want to stay with companies that have great reputations. They want to be involved with something bigger than themselves where they feel they can make a difference. This is especially true of millennials. They want to work for organizations that are not just profit-focused. And they tend to stay with organizations that have strong, aligned values and plenty of developmental opportunities.

Leadership Questions about Your Brand

Every leader should be able to answer the following three questions:

» How would you describe your organization's brand?

» How would your team members describe your organization's brand?

» How would your customers describe your organization's brand?

Leaders learn to understand the answers to these questions in order to position, improve, and grow your brand. When leaders understand these answers, they can make adjustments to improve the brand or to leverage a positive brand to maximize productivity and profits.

Conclusion

"The only thing of real importance that leaders do is to create and change culture."

–**Edgar Schein**

Senior leaders interact and collaborate with the entire organization to build and sustain a strong brand and culture. It is their responsibility to enable cultural change and also to improve the culture.

Your culture should be clear and defined. Your culture and your brand can be strong competitive advantages because of how difficult they are to copy. When you have a competitive cultural advantage, your organization can thrive. Your revenues and productivity will increase.

Employees, especially millennials, stay with companies that have strong, aligned values and developmental opportunities. A strong organizational culture can result in high retention and engagement rates.

It is vital that new hires be culturally good fits, meaning that their beliefs, values, and behaviors are well aligned with the culture. If they are not, the employees will cause damage to the culture and eventually become disengaged. Leaders cannot make the mistake of hiring cultural misfits, and if they do, the misfits should be terminated quickly.

Ask yourself the following questions about your company's culture and brand:

» How would I describe my organization's culture?

» Which characteristics of a strong culture does my organization possess?

» If my organization's culture needs to be reshaped, what needs to change and how will I help the organization do it?

» What are several competitive advantages of my organization's culture?

» How would I describe my organization's brand?

» How am I leveraging my organization's brand and culture to engage, retain, and hire top talent?

10

The Perfect Leadership Triad: Creating a Strong Leadership Culture

*T*he definition of "triad" is "a group or set of three connected things."

Establishing a strong people-focused, coaching-centered, and performance-driven leadership approach comprises what I call *The Perfect Leadership Triad*. All three elements are required in order for you to have a strong leadership culture. The culture is not complete if you leave out one of these elements.

So, what does The Perfect Leadership Triad look like? It starts with recognizing that your business is driven by your employees. They interface with the customers. Without them you are only an empty shell of a company.

As mentioned previously, most organizations do not put their people first. It may be because they do not believe in their people or have not trained and coached them to be effective. Or maybe they believe that the product or service can sell itself on its own merits. Perhaps they believe that management can already get everything they need out of their people, regardless of how it treats them. Or maybe they believe that the top leaders are the ones driving the business solely through their brilliant leadership and business acumen. They may believe that people will respond by simply being told what to do.

In many organizations, there is no attempt to win the hearts and the minds of the employees. People are not coached and developed, with the result that eventually they will become disenchanted and leave. They will also leave if their loyalty to the company is not reciprocated. This may be one of the reasons that, according to Gallup polls, about 70 percent of employees feel disengaged at work.

Understand Why the Company Exists: Simon Says…

"All organizations start with WHY, but only the great ones keep their WHY clear year after year."

–Simon Sinek

So how do you create, establish, and maintain a people-focused, performance-driven, and coaching-centered culture? The answer is to understand why your company exists and then to do everything you and the other leaders can do to inspire your employees to believe in its purpose and live its values.

Author Simon Sinek said, "Very few people or companies can clearly articulate WHY they do WHAT they do. When I say WHY, I don't mean to make money—that's a result. By WHY I mean what is your purpose, cause or belief? WHY does your company exist? WHY do you get out of bed every morning? And WHY should anyone care?"

Obviously, the founders of most companies set forth and established the core values and purpose of the company. Most likely the founders also articulated and lived the Why of the company. So, organizations must go back and understand why the company even exists.

This all starts with truly living the values of your company. No organization can establish a strong culture in a vacuum. It is created and lived by senior leaders who evince a passion for the values of the company.

The CEO is the keeper and teacher of the Why. Her primary duty is to create an environment where employees at all levels feel great about their daily work and about the company.

Senior and midlevel leaders are responsible for the What. They execute against the strategies and the Why of the company. Strong leaders leave the How to their people.

Senior leaders are effective at communicating why the organization exists and why its employees should be excited and energized every day to live the culture. Leaders provide insight and communicate the purpose of the organization.

Employees understand their roles and how they impact organizational performance. The culture needs to appeal to the employees. If an employee is not energized by the culture or does not live its values, she is not a good fit. She should be removed and replaced with an employee who does fit the culture.

As we have discussed earlier, it is vital that companies hire employees who fit the culture. Poor hiring decisions will be the downfall of any culture, especially if such hiring mistakes are made at senior leadership levels.

Likewise, if companies do not really understand their reason for existing or do not comprehend and live their core values, employees will feel confused and unsatisfied. In my experience, most companies are good at articulating vision and mission statements, though few truly live them. Most statements were created through exercises that did not focus on the core values and the Why of the company.

Novo Nordisk: Examplar of The Perfect Leadership Triad

During the tenure of its former CEO, Lars Rebien Sørensen, Novo Nordisk was a great example of The Perfect Leadership Triad. The organization's culture focused on people, coaching, and performance.

As noted earlier, the Novo Nordisk culture was consistent around the world. An employee in China lived the same values, experienced the same purpose, and enjoyed the same culture as an employee in Denmark or the United States.

At Novo Nordisk, one of the things that Andy Ajello implemented was a Look and Feel policy for the sales force that affected the entire biopharmaceutical industry. This was a change in the dress code that allowed sales representatives to dress like the customer. For example, instead of wearing high-priced suits, representatives dressed in business casual.

By doing so, they did not stand out from the patients in offices or give the appearance that their medications were priced high because of fancy biopharmaceutical sales forces.

Coaching and developing people were key priorities, beginning with the executive management team and extending all the way down to first-line managers. In the United States, the sales force led by former senior vice president of sales Andy Ajello was out in front with coaching. Sales vice presidents, directors, and first-line managers were focused on creating and living a coaching culture. Several directors and talent management leaders completed certifications to become executive coaches in an effort to be more effective.

Leaders and employees at all levels were motivated and accountable for their job responsibilities and goals. It was observed that employees loved what they were doing and felt passionate about the impact they had on improving patients' lives.

As a result of Novo Nordisk's focus on people and coaching, performance reached the highest level in company history.

As Novo Nordisk's fairly new CEO, Lars Fruergaard Jørgensen is faced with the challenge of maintaining the culture established by his predecessor. With new challenges in the marketplace and business pressures, aspects of his business such as people management, effective coaching, and performance will be even more vital.

The Chicken or the Egg?

Which comes first in an organization? Is it people, coaching, or performance?

A people-focused strategy, especially when it is combined with coaching, will result in better performance. You can't believe in being people-focused without providing employees coaching, opportunities to develop, and the autonomy to decide how to do things. Bottom line: the most effective way to manage the development and performance of the employee is through effective coaching.

So, what happens when you combine a people-focused approach with coaching? It results in increased performance and heightened revenues, especially when leaders hold employees accountable for performance.

I believe that most leaders and organizations do not consistently hold employees accountable for performance. Many companies speak about performance, but few can actually establish or sustain a performance-driven culture. I believe it is because the focus is on the business and numbers rather than on the people. But why *do* companies have problems differentiating between people and business? It is usually because they are typically focused on short-term numbers, resulting from pressure from investors, especially those on Wall Street.

Think for a moment about the Costco example, discussed earlier. Although Costco had strong performance, Wall Street wanted it to cut employees' salaries and benefits. But the

Costco CEO, Craig Jelinek, knew this short-term outlook would devastate the people-focused, coaching-centered, and performance-driven culture he had carefully created over years. Instead, he stayed focused on living the Costco culture through his decision *not* to try to satisfy Wall Street.

How do you think the thousands of Costco employees felt when they saw the company's values remain intact? Certainly, Jelinek's response to the pressures of Wall Street sent a clear signal to all employees that Costco leadership was not going to devalue the culture or change its priorities.

As we have seen from the research conducted by Lindsay McGregor and Neel Doshi, leaders understand what motivates each employee. When employees are motivated by the culture and the work, you will see improvements in revenue, cost, risk, and customer satisfaction. (Lindsay McGregor and Neel Doshi, "How Company Culture Shapes Employee Motivation," *Harvard Business Review,* November 25, 2015, https://hbr.org/2015/11/how-company-culture-shapes-employee-motivation)

Coaching-centered leadership leads to a people-focused and performance-driven culture. When leaders effectively coach their employees, they build trust and goodwill. They set an expectation that leaders should help employees reach and even exceed company goals. Great Leader Coaches understand that it's people who drive performance. By placing employees at the center of the corporate strategy and culture, companies establish a competitive advantage that is difficult to copy.

Which Comes First, Employees or Customers?

Peter Drucker, one of the foremost authorities on business, was considered the founder of modern management. He contributed enormously to the philosophical and practical foundations of the modern business corporation. He is famous for having said, "The purpose of a business is to create (and keep) a customer." He also stated, simply: "A company's primary responsibility is to serve its customers."

According to Drucker, without customers a company simply cannot survive. So, in almost all situations the customer needs to come first, as the customer can always choose to take his business elsewhere. According to Drucker, the customer is the company's top priority.

Now let's compare this belief with that of Richard Branson, who stated, "If you take care of your employees, they will take care of the clients." Branson does *not* put the customer first. Employees are his company's top priority. When employees are placed first, in his view, they will help make happy customers.

"It should go without saying, if the person who works at your company is 100 percent proud of the brand and you give them the tools to do a good job and they are treated well, they're going to be happy," Branson told *Inc.* president and editor-in-chief Eric Schurenberg in an interview.

"As Branson sees it, the formula is very simple: Happy employees equal happy customers. Similarly, an unhappy employee can ruin the brand experience for not just one, but numerous customers. According to Branson, his priorities are: employees first, customers second, and shareholders third." (Mark Norige,Board Forum, July 2016, www.theboardforum.com)

There is a delicate balance between being people-focused and customer-centric. Organizations that create strong people-focused leadership cultures are far more likely to be customer-centric.

As a leading business consultant concludes, "A collection collection of highly talented employees without purpose or direction is pointless. A collection of customers without anyone working to meet their needs is a missed opportunity. Employees without customers is pointless. The real challenge lies with a company's leaders to recruit and motivate able employees to meet and exceed customer needs." (Mark Norige, Principal, Consultant, and Chief Catalyst of the Board Forum, July 2016, www.theboardforum.com)

Conclusion

As I have stated throughout this book, I believe that the most successful companies are those that focus on people, coaching, and performance. Their strategies and culture include all three elements of my Perfect Leadership Triad.

Great organizations always put employees before customers, because it is the employees, especially front-line ones, who interface with customers, solve their problems, and sell them products or solutions.

Numerous studies cited throughout the book have demonstrated that it is coaching that has the greatest impact on increasing productivity, performance, and revenue. The coaching should be focused on performance and on people development. Coaching engages employees and makes them want to stay with the organization.

High-performing organizations have learned how to develop, coach, and train employees to drive performance. They have mastered the processes of achieving goals and exceeding performance expectations.

Ask yourself these questions about being a leader who follows the principles of The Perfect Leadership Triad:

>> What is the purpose of my team and organization?

>> Which comes first for me, employees or customers?

>> What are the benefits of being a people-focused leader?

>> What are the benefits of being a coaching-centered leader?

>> What are the benefits of being a performance-driven leader?

>> What do I need to do more of (or less of) to be a leader who follows the principles of The Perfect Leadership Triad?

Conclusion

Key Principles of The Perfect Leadership Triad

People-Focused Leadership

"Everyone always talks about building a relationship with your customer. I think you build one with your employees first."

–Angela Ahrendts, *Senior Vice President, Apple*

When people know you care about and respect them, they will buy into your vision, be happier, and therefore become more engaged and work harder for you. As we have seen, happy employees mean happy customers!

Coaching-Centered Leadership

"Everybody needs a coach."

–Bill Gates

Coaching is the cornerstone of every great leader. Leaders who coach effectively develop and inspire their employees to be more productive. Coaching is the one action that will drive the business more than any other activity.

Leader Coach

"People buy into the leader before they buy into the vision."

–John Maxwell

THE PERFECT LEADERSHIP TRIAD

The Leader Coach recognizes the role of coaching in her success as a leader. If a leader does not coach effectively, she will not grow the business at the rate necessary to sustain long-term success.

Performance-Driven Leadership

> *"The true measure of the value of any business leader and manager is performance."*
>
> **–Brian Tracy**

No leader can sustain long-term performance if it comes at the expense of employees. This does not mean that a leader has to be beloved; but she *does* need to be trustworthy, transparent, and candid with her employees. She demonstrates that she cares about her employees enough to hold them accountable. She coaches for performance.

Hire the Right People and Keep Them Engaged

> *"The best leader is the one who has sense enough to pick good men to do what he wants done, and the self-restraint to keep from meddling with them while they do it."*
>
> **–Theodore Roosevelt**

As we have seen, it is critical to hire for cultural fit. Skills can be taught but cultural fit cannot be learned. Leaders cannot afford to hire the wrong people. When a leader makes a hiring mistake, she corrects it quickly. The leader cannot wait for the employee to leave. She coaches the employee up or out of the organization.

What is worse than an employee who quits and leaves? One who quits and stays! Gallup polls have consistently demonstrated that about 70 percent of employees are disengaged.

One survey reported by McKinsey showed that "73% of employees are thinking about another job and that 43% were more likely to consider a new one than they had been a year earlier." (Scott Keller and Mary Meaner, "Attracting and Retaining the Right Talent," McKinsey, 2016, https://www. mckinsey.com/business-functions/organization/our-insights/ attracting-and-retaining-the-right-talent)

Engagement is greatly improved when leaders focus on people, coaching, and performance. Remember, people want to work for companies that share their values.

Leaders Set the Tone

"Ultimately, it's on the company leaders to set the tone.... Not only the CEO, but the leaders across the company. If you select them so carefully that they then hire the right people, it's a nice self-fulfilling prophecy."

–Tim Cook, *CEO, Apple*

Leaders, especially senior leaders, not only help set the culture, establish the corporate brand, and demonstrate that people and coaching are critical. They also set a tone across the entire organization that greatly affects all employees.

The most important thing leaders do is hire employees who are high-performers and who fit the culture. When the right people are on the team, great things happen.

A Final Word...

I have given you much of the knowledge and many of the secrets I have amassed in my professional life, to help you become a great leader. You came to this book to learn and to maximize your leadership competencies.

When I started writing this book, one of my goals was to help leaders like you believe how critical employees are to your business. I want you to feel confident that putting employees before the business not only is the right thing to do, but it will also help you enjoy long-term success.

Another goal for this book was to prove to you the benefits of coaching your employees. As you have seen throughout, coaching engenders trust with your employees while increasing performance and revenues. Although I am a former Fortune 500 executive, and a trained, credentialed executive coach, I am *still* learning how to be a more effective coach!

I hope that I have proven that high-performing leaders care enough about their employees to hold them accountable for performance. Performance comes through people and through coaching.

I dream of a day when all leaders are people-focused, coaching-centered, and performance-driven. The business world would be a far better place, employees would be more engaged and more productive, and organizations would be more profitable.

If this is also *your* aspiration and belief, let's work together to help you become a leader who focuses on people, coaching, and performance.

Get to the Next Level of Leadership

If you want to learn to become a more effective people-focused, coaching-centered, and performance-driven leader, I am here to help you. Whether you would like one-on-one or team coaching, leadership development workshops that focus on the principles behind The Perfect Leadership Triad, or a stimulating a keynote speaker, I can help you.

Please reach out to me at **eric@turbivillegroup.com** so that you can become a more effective leader.

TurbivilleGroup
PEOPLE | COACHING | PERFORMANCE

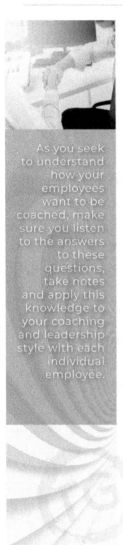

As you seek to understand how your employees want to be coached, make sure you listen to the answers to these questions, take notes and apply this knowledge to your coaching and leadership style with each individual employee.

How I Want to be Coached

How do you determine how employees want to be coached? You ask them! This tool will help your employees clarify and share their needs and expectations while in a coaching relationship with you, their direct reports, or their peers.

The one thing I need most from my coach is:

_____

_____

Many things motivate me; however, my top three motivators are:

_____

_____

_____

When you are coaching me, you can realistically expect me to:

_____

_____

_____

I need and expect my coach to:

_____

_____

_____

Your support for me can best be shown by:

_____

_____

_____

Some developmental opportunities that you could assist me with are:

_____

_____

_____

Additional information that is important while coaching me is:

_____

_____

_____

Considering my past managers/coaches, I'd like you to:

Stop :_____

Start :_____

Continue :_____

TurbivilleGroup
PEOPLE | COACHING | PERFORMANCE

It is critical that you act on the feedback received in the Stay Interview.

Not only will you build trust with your employees, you will show that you are listening and taking action.

Stay Interview

Do you know why employees stay with your organization? Have you ever asked your employees why they stay with your organization? You might be surprised at the answers. I have found that a Stay Interview is a gateway into the minds of your employees that will shed light on what you are doing right and what you can improve. Here are the questions you should ask each employee:

What do you like most about working here?
_____
_____

What keeps you working here?
_____
_____

What do you like least about working here?
_____
_____

What can we do to make your experience at work better?
_____
_____

If you could change something about your job, what would that be?
_____
_____

Which of your talents are not being used in your current role?
_____
_____

What would you like to learn here?
_____
_____

What can I do as your leader to best support you?
_____
_____

What can I do more of or less of as your leader?
_____
_____

If you owned or led this company (team), what would you change?
_____
_____

What Motivates Me

If you are to be successful as a leader, you must understand how to inspire and mobilize your team. The only way you can do this effectively is to understand what motivates each of your people. The best way to find out what motivates employees is to ask them and then listen! Here are some questions that you can ask your employees to understand what motivates them:

What part of your current job do you enjoy most?

_____

_____

What part of your current job frustrates you the most?

_____

_____

What part of your current job gives you the greatest sense of purpose?

_____

_____

When are your contributions to the organization's overall goals most inspiring?

_____

_____

I define my purpose as: (In other words, I go to work because I want to:)

_____

_____

How often does your leader recognize and reward you for your job performance?

_____

_____

What type of reward do you find the most motivating?

_____

_____

What does reaching your full potential look like? How can I help you achieve it?

_____

_____

What have past leaders done to inspire you?

_____

_____

The sidebar reads: Remember you cannot motivate anyone. All you can do is inspire them based on their individual motivators. Leaders don't motivate, they inspire!

Acknowledgments

As a leader, I love to help people grow, develop, and feel inspired to do their best work and live their best life. There is nothing I like more than to see people succeed and achieve the things that they want to accomplish.

There are so many people who have supported me and taught me how to be a great leader. They range from family, friends, business associates, and religious leaders. The list is long, and I apologize that I cannot include everyone.

I want to thank my wife, Randa, my best friend and the love of my life, and my children, Kelsey, Eric, Chase, Aidan, and Zoe, who supported me through this somewhat time-consuming adventure. Their support means the world to me. To my mom, Barbara, who taught me the value of learning and fueled my passion for reading and working hard to be a good person. To my sister, Stephanie, who follows her passion every day and is a shining example of a breast cancer survivor. To my brother, Jimmy, who passed away a few years ago from the ravishing effects of diabetes.

Thank you to the great leaders whom I had in my corporate career. I was fortunate to have learned from many strong leaders who exemplified the principles found in this book. Without your examples, I would be half the leader that I became. Thanks to the people who worked with and for me. I am sure that I learned more from you than I taught you.

Thank you to Göran Ando, Steve Sosland, Andy Ajello, Tim Edwards, Milton Goggans, Scott Eblin, and Tom Ori for your input, feedback, support, and coaching as I wrote the book. I know how busy you are as executives and leaders, and I greatly appreciate that you took the time to do it.

Thanks to my editor, Mark Woodworth, who reminded me of proper grammar and sentence structure as he edited the book. My book coaches, John Eggen and Christy Tryhus, were instrumental in helping me complete this book.

Many authors, leaders, and books have inspired and taught me key leadership principles. Some whose works and thinking come to mind are Peter Drucker, Richard Branson, Malcolm Gladwell, Jim Collins, and Marcus Buckingham

Some of my favorite books are: *Results-Based Leadership,* by Dave Ulrich, Jack Zenger, and Norm Smallwood; *The 7 Habits of Highly Effective People,* by Stephen Covey; *The Four Agreements,* by Don Miguel Ruiz; *Executive Coaching with Backbone and Heart,* by Mary Beth O'Neill; *The One Thing,* by Gary Keller; *Start with Why,* by Simon Sinek; *Getting to Yes,* by Roger Fisher and William Ury; *Leadership and Self-Deception,* by The Arbinger Institute; *The Effective Executive,* by Peter Drucker; *DRiVE,* by Daniel Pink; *The Innovator's Solution,* by Clayton Christensen and Michael Raynor; *Stand Out,* by Dorie Clark; *Judgment in Managerial Decision-Making,* by Max Bazerman; and *The Next Level,* by Scott Eblin. The most important lessons I have learned about leadership, however, have come from the scriptures.

I appreciate all the feedback I received on the content of this book. The leaders who read the prepublication version of this book truly affected how I communicated my fundamental beliefs about leadership in this book.

Finally, I want to thank all those who will read this book and apply its principles, which I believe can inspire many people to achieve their leadership dreams. As you put these principles to good use, I hope your example shines a light on how important people are, and how coaching can help them grow, develop, and perform at a higher level. Thank you in advance for passing this book on to other leaders!

Index

Z

Transformational Leadership and Coaching Program

Do you seek to become a more impactful, effective executive? Do you want to maximize your productivity and the performance of your team? If so, I can help you achieve it through the Transformational Leadership and Coaching Program (TLC). This is a 6-month, customizable, executive leadership program that combines in-person, hands-on learning, with virtual, individualized 1:1 and group coaching for 6 to 12 executives.

The TLC program is intended for both experienced and transitioning executives, as well as for high-potential leaders. My program is practical and includes pre-assessments, training, individual and mastermind group coaching, follow-up, real-world application, and final assessments.

My Transformational Leadership and Coaching Program will not only positively impact your leaders to be more productive and higher performers, but it will also influence your culture so that you can engage and retain key employees. I believe in training leaders to be people-focused, coaching-centered, and performance-driven. By doing so, they will increase performance, engage and retain employees, and create happy customers.

Make the decision today to focus on people, coaching, and performance. Let me help!

Please contact me to schedule a free, 30-minute strategy session to discuss how this program can help your leaders and organization.

I can be reached at eric@turbivillegroup.com or www.turbivillegroup.com.

1:1 or Team Executive Coaching

Do you feel overwhelmed with your leadership responsibilities? Do you feel pressure to improve the performance of your team?

What is the quickest way to improve your effectiveness and performance as an executive? *Coaching!* Whether you need 1:1 executive coaching, or would like me to coach your team, or both, I can help you.

With my many years of coaching, my experience as a former Fortune 500 executive, and the research I conducted for this book, *The Perfect Leadership Triad,* I will provide you with practical insights and a pragmatic approach to become a more-effective executive. I will coach and develop you to ensure that you maximize the productivity of your team.

I bring clarity to executives so that you can maximize your leadership performance.

Whether you are a new, emerging, or experienced leader, I meet you where you are in your career—and help take you to where you want to go. It's what I do!

Make the decision today to develop and grow your leadership competencies. Let me help you!

Please contact me to schedule a free, 30-minute strategic discovery session to discuss how coaching can help your leaders and organization.

I can be reached at eric@turbivillegroup.com or www.turbivillegroup.com.

Leadership Development Programs

Whether you want to learn how to build and develop a higher-performing team or wish to master the principles of *The Perfect Leadership Triad,* I can help.

My leadership programs focus on helping you become a more-effective and productive leader. These transformational programs are not just one-time events. I do follow-ups for three months with 1:1 or team coaching so that you have assistance in applying the principles you learn in your real-life work environment.

Here are three off-the-shelf leadership programs that I offer:

1. The Perfect Leadership Triad: How to Maximize Productivity through People, Coaching, and Performance

2. Leader Coach: How You Can Become an Elite Coach so Your Team Consistently Exceeds Expectations

3. Building and Leading a High-Performing Team

Make the decision today to develop and grow into a stronger, more-productive leader. Let me help you!

Please contact me to schedule a free, 30-minute strategy session to discuss how these leadership development programs can help your leaders and organization.

I can be reached at eric@turbivillegroup.com or www.turbivillegroup.com.

Keynote Speaker

I have spoken to many small and large groups, ranging from 10 to 1,000 people. I bring high energy to my speaking engagements because I am passionate about the leadership principles that I wrote about in my book, *The Perfect Leadership Triad: How Top Executives Maximize Productivity through People, Coaching, and Performance.*

I work with you before the meeting to ensure that my talk meets both your team's needs and your own expectations. I share insights and relevant, real-life stories about leadership. My speaking approach is practical, and the principles I speak about can be applied immediately.

Based on your specific needs, I can teach attendees how to maximize productivity through focusing on their people, developing into elite coaches, and setting high-performance standards. With over 20 years of personal leadership and coaching experience, I help your leaders focus on what drives productivity and peak performance.

You can choose from one of my four keynote addresses:

1. Why Employees Matter

2. The Perfect Leadership Triad: How to Maximize Productivity through People, Coaching, and Performance

3. The Leader Coach: How You Can Become an Elite Coach So Your Team Consistently Exceeds Expectations

4. Building and Leading a High-Performing Team

If you are interested in having an inspiring and actionable keynote talk, book me to speak to your team.

Please contact me to schedule a free, 30-minute strategy session to discuss your organization's needs and goals for your next meeting.

I can be reached at eric@turbivillegroup.com or www.turbivillegroup.com.

Why Work with Eric Turbiville?

I am in the 1%...

While there are almost 50,000 executive coaches, only about 1% have been Fortune 500 executives. When you work with me, you will be working with a former Fortune 500 executive. When you select an executive coach and leadership development expert, you want a leader who has experienced similar opportunities and challenges.

I can help you accelerate your performance and professional growth. The business world needs your leadership. Come on this journey as I help you drive and sustain high performance!

If you want to become an elite executive, let's work together!

To contact Eric Turbiville, go to **www.turbivillegroup.com**.

Follow his leadership blog at **www.turbivillegroup.com**.

ERIC TURBIVILLE is an accelerator of performance and professional growth. He is a credentialed executive coach, author, keynote speaker, and president of the Turbiville Group, a leadership development and coaching firm that specializes in helping organizations transform their executives into higher-performing leaders. He is a former Fortune 500 executive who has coached experienced, transitioning, and high-potential executives in many large companies. Turbiville holds an MBA degree from Brigham Young University and is credentialed as a Professional Certified Coach (PCC) through the International Coaching Federation.

To contact Eric Turbiville, go to **www.turbivillegroup.com**. Follow his leadership blog at **www.turbivillegroup.com**. Cover design: Junar Delmo Anino

TG Publishing